A MOSAIC OF MUSINGS

Daily Thoughts for People on the Way

A MOSAIC OF MUSINGS

Daily Thoughts for People on the Way

KENNETH J. DALE

Kirk House Publishers
Minneapolis, Minnesota

A MOSAIC OF MUSINGS
Daily Thoughts for People on the Way

KENNETH J. DALE

Book design: Mary Stoddard
Paintings: Kenneth J. Dale

ISBN - 13: 978-1-933794-33-4
ISBN - 10: 1-933794-33-X

LCCN: 2010939046

Kirk House Publishers, PO Box 390759, Minneapolis, MN 55439
www.kirkhouse.com • 1-888-696-1828
Manufactured in the United States of America.

*I dedicate this book to all who join me
in seeking the Way, remembering that
"'If with all your heart you truly seek me,
you will surely find me' says the Lord."
(Jeremiah 29:13)*

Contents

These topics are not treated in consecutive order,
but they constitute the contents of this book.
See the Index for a full list of all the pieces and their location.

Preface

I welcome the reader to walk with me through a year of devotional thoughts that, hopefully, will provide some fresh perspectives on the Christian faith. My hope and prayer is, through questioning and probing, to make our faith richer and deeper.

I did not undertake this project with the intention of "writing a book." Like my previous book, *A Seeker's Journal* (Kirk House Publishers, 2003), these paragraphs have been written piece by piece over a period of time "as the Spirit leads." They are thoughts that probe into the meaning of some essential aspects of Christian faith. They are personal thoughts; they are not the result of research, other than research into my own soul.

Being aware of this orientation to the book, the reader cannot expect logical, consistent development of themes. You must, rather, expect to find some inconsistencies and paradoxical statements. That reflects my approach to life, and to theology, both of which are seasoned with ambiguities and paradoxes.

I believe that truth is not something to be contained in a neat box full of well ordered statements. Truth is rather like the flashes of reflected light on a wall, coming from a diamond that we cannot see. These flashes sparkle brightly, then dim away, and present a wonderful array of different colors. If you, the reader, can get in this mind set, then we can walk together for a year enjoying the lights as we go.

This book is not for those already satisfied with their understanding of faith. This is for those who peek into the Christian world, wondering what it's all about. This is also for mature Christians who have questions about the deeper meaning of beliefs they have taken for granted all their life. This is for life-long seekers, like myself.

The author

We might feel more at home with each other as we take this walk if you know a few things about who I am and how I came to think the way I do. I was born into a Midwest rural family in Nebraska in 1926. My parents and we three brothers were nurtured in the local Lutheran Church in the tradition of Scandinavian orthodoxy and piety. After seminary education and ordination into the ministry of the Lutheran Church, my wife Eloise and I were called to serve the Lutheran Church in Japan, which we did, mainly as pastor and professor at the Lutheran College and Seminary in Tokyo for our entire career. We were blessed with two sons, nurtured and educated in Japan.

During that time I did doctoral work at Union Seminary in New York, writing a dissertation on a Japanese Buddhist sect. I consider my work as founder and director of the Personal Growth and Counseling Center in Tokyo to be my main service to Japan.

Since retirement in 1996 we have lived at a retirement community in Claremont, California, called Pilgrim Place. This is an intentional, inter-denominational community of people who have given their lives in various kinds of religious service. It is a community characterized by intense concern and activism regarding social problems from a Christian perspective.

One does not go through life untouched by the influence of social and ideological environment. Some of the strong influences on my life and thought, in addition to early background—which is always decisive—have been study at Union Seminary, living in a non-Christian society for 45 years, experience with Buddhism, listening as a counselor to the problems of countless individuals, both Japanese and Westerners, and the life style of Pilgrim Place during the past 14 years. This thumb nail sketch might give you a clue as to why you will perceive the multi-faceted character of my faith rather than a neat box of unchanging truths.

Format

Now a few words of orientation about the arrangement of this book. It is in the format of daily readings for one year. However, it is not a 365 day year, but consists of five days a week (you get weekends off!) for four weeks each of the twelve months. I have chosen this format because I would like you, the reader, to "nibble at" just one thought a day and hopefully reflect on it and either affirm or contradict it in your own way. You will get indigestion if you try to read many pages in one sitting!

You will discover that the pieces are not arranged haphazardly. Generally speaking, each of the days of the week has an over-all topic. The early part of the week presents theological, and the latter part more personal ideas. I.e., Mondays are about God, Tuesdays about Jesus Christ, Wednesdays are usually on the Holy Spirit, church, or scripture, Thursdays usually on human responses to God, especially through prayer and the Christian way of life, while Fridays are reflections on many and various topics of living.

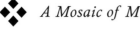

I do not pretend that this volume presents a balanced view of the Christian faith or theological themes. I have my own interests and foci, which will become evident to the reader after a couple of months of readings.

In particular, you will notice that a great many of the Tuesday readings regarding Christ are "The Cross event," which indicates my special interest in how we should interpret the whole event of the suffering and crucifixion of Jesus in connection with human salvation. This has been a consuming point of interest for me ever since writing a ThM dissertation on the topic at Princeton Seminary. You will discover that my conclusions differ from most of the traditional interpretations.

Two other topics have drawn me into endless inquiry and exploration. One is the topic that appears on Mondays, viz., the nature of the divine Being. I am constrained continually to inquire about the nature of the Holy One, who nevertheless continually eludes me. But what is more important in any religious quest than trying to touch the hem of the garment of the One we call "God"?

Another topic that you will find repeatedly appearing is the Lord's Prayer. That brief prayer is for me the ever-expanding pathway to communication with God, whom Jesus called "Father." This prayer has been the model for infinitely rich and suggestive prayer throughout my life.

The general topic for each day is indicated in italics at the beginning of the piece, followed by a more specific title for each. There is a brief Table of Contents that indicates recurring themes, and for the sake of readers who might want to follow through on certain topics, I have created an Index that indicates the page numbers where certain topics are dealt with.

The Pictures

You will find pictures on each of the twelve pages indicating the month that follows (First Month, Second Month, etc.). Unfortunately, black and white had to be substituted for the original colors. They are my gift to the reader, to add a bit of variety as you open the book. I started painting for my own pleasure after taking a class last year taught by Eleanor Scott Meyers, a Pilgrim Place resident. This has been a new adventure for me. I make no pretense of being a skilled artist; I simply paint as my imagination leads me. A few are realistic, most are abstract; some utilize Japanese characters as a theme. I hope they don't distract from the otherwise serious content of this writing!

The picture on the front cover was painted as a hint of a stained glass window, showing several Christian symbols. I chose it for the cover because the feeling of the picture matches the word "Mosaic."

Kenneth J. Dale
540 West Eighth Street
Claremont, CA 91711

First Month

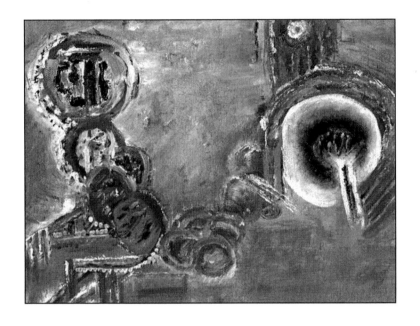

Circles—no beginning, no ending
Oil, 2009

God is with us

The mystery of God is that we believe God is always "with us." This is the Bible's message. And yet—life goes on. Day after day is ho-hum, hum-drum "business as usual." Bad things continually happen to good people; people of sincere faith pray earnestly but nothing happens. No one has ever seen this God who is supposed to be always "with us."

How do we make sense of this, in a way that shows our faith is not just stupid naiveté and in the end only an illusion? I think it forces us to rethink the nature of the Divine, of the God who is always "with us." If life is 98% hum-drum while at the same time we believe God is with us, then God must be part of, integrated into the hum-drum itself.

Normal people can handle the hum-drum aspects of life themselves. We don't need a revelation of special divine power to help us brush our teeth, or drive to work. So God must be right there in the hum-drum, the dynamic process of the hum-drum itself.

Yet we immediately recognize that God is more than hum-drum. If this were not so, it would have been both impossible and unnecessary for God to reveal the divine Self in various ways throughout history. Marcus Borg expresses a meaningful insight when he says that God is "the more" in all the phenomena of our lives.

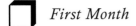

The Apostles' Creed: what it says; what it doesn't say

This classic creedal statement of Christian belief skips the life and teachings of Jesus. Why? Often we are critical of this. But some have taken a different approach to that Creed: What is essential in Trinitarian faith is not the teaching of Jesus, but the Incarnation as such. St. Paul saw the mystery of the eternal divine plan as Incarnation and Redemption.

Jesus was not just a great teacher, nor even a great healer. He was a manifestation of God in our midst, and that is what his contemporaries could not understand or tolerate. To confess our faith in this is the great leap of Christian faith, but this is what we affirm in the Apostles' Creed.

Although we believe in the complete humanity of Jesus, there is something cosmic about Christ and his death and his resurrection. For it speaks of the power of evil in the world, and promises new life to all the world through the resurrection. This is the focus of the Apostles' Creed.

Reality of Spirit

Atheists, agnostics and those who live by the world view of science that says only the material is real, deny the existence of God because there is no visible evidence that this unseen Being exists. But this is a strangely unreasonable notion. So much we experience in the world and in ourselves cannot be seen.

Take just two things: One is air. Air is absolutely invisible but absolutely real. We feel how it expands our lungs with every breath we take, and without it, in just a few minutes we are dead. And it is air that supports the giant air buses transporting hundreds of passengers five miles above our heads.

The other is the reality of "spirit" as we experience it in our own being. Feelings and emotions, memory, the ability to plan, the power to reason, imagination—these constitute our invisible nature that we call "spirit." This essence of human nature is completely non-material, even though it is mysteriously connected to the flesh of the brain. So why should there not be a spirit in the universe as well as in my body?—a spirit that is loving, creative and powerful, and so mysterious that we write it with a capital S—the Spirit. Yes, I believe in the Holy Spirit!

Have courage to face yourself!

In the time of prayer we stand before our Maker. The time of prayer forces us to be honest in facing ourselves, our deepest motivations and goals. That's why praying is never an easy task. It would be so much easier simply to act as a puppet, using body and brain to do the jobs set before us or the jobs put upon us by others, without bothering with introspection.

We resist praying because we resist facing ourselves. To stop and be quiet and reflect and intentionally ask the Higher Power for something, using the will and imagination as well as the intellect—that is work! This is the natural resistance of my superficial self toward the deeper realization of my own self. By nature I hesitate to face myself and its ultimate goals and meaning. I fear what might appear in an honest encounter. My own inadequacy and waywardness might loom large. Or the challenge of a calling to rise up and do a job might be revealed to me.

Perhaps this is why, when it comes time to pray, we prefer to settle for a standard written prayer. May God give us courage to say an honest prayer today!

Questions enrich us

Mark Hansen, Presiding Bishop of the Evangelical Lutheran Church in America, once wrote the following regarding questioning our faith:

"Questions invite us to contemplate the mystery of being human. They become the occasion for deepening faith and expanding understanding. Lively questions enrich the community of believers as we invite people to Christ and work for justice and peace." (The Lutheran, March, 2002)

His point is that people of faith should take a stance of asking provocative questions, continually seeking for truth. I try to do that, and that's why I have felt compelled to write these humble fragments, questioning tradition, but with the hope of strengthening faith.

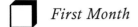

Elusive time and space

What is more intriguing than reflecting on the reality of
time and space? Both of these concepts are absolutely
indescribable and incomprehensible. What is time? It is
outside the range of the senses. It is nothing. I only know
that the earth spins on its axis causing light and darkness
as we face the sun and turn away from it, and that I
occasionally get hungry and sleepy. But none of these
things have anything to do with time itself. "Eternity"
is often contrasted with "time," but eternity is still more
elusive than time.

   And what is space? It does not exist either. I know that
two objects are not in the same place at the same time, and
that there is an "in between." That is what we call "space."
But there is no substance or entity that we can point to and
say, There is "space."

   All we can know about time and space is that we have set
up arbitrary methods of measuring the stuff called "time,"
and measuring the stuff called "space." But just because we
have certain scales of measurements, does not mean that
we know the reality of what time and space are.

   But we say that God is "eternal," and that God is in
"heaven." Both of these concepts defy our grasp of time
and space. How long is "eternity"? Where is "heaven"?
These are pointers toward the mystery of God and our
existence after death.

Second Week   Tuesday   *Jesus Christ*

The essence of Christian belief

The 24th chapter of Matthew's Gospel—the judgment scene where Jesus separates the sheep and the goats, i.e., separates people on the basis of their works of compassion—proclaims clearly what it means to believe in Christ. It is to be committed to the "Jesus-way" of life; the way of loving compassion for all.

Belief is not intellectual assent to certain doctrines about Jesus, e.g., the substitutionary theory of the atonement which focuses on the Cross as a vicarious sacrifice on our behalf so that God's wrath would be appeased so he could forgive our sins.

Is it being sacrilegious to suggest that Jesus could probably care less about what doctrine of atonement we hold, because "belief" is not so much assent to a way of thinking as it is committing ourselves to and participating in the "Jesus-way" of life.

Jesus, walk beside me on the way of compassion this day.

The Spirit gives gifts

When I pray, "Come Holy Spirit"—that prayer which Jesus said would always be answered—or ask God for the gift of the Spirit, what do I actually expect? Something like talking in tongues? I think not.

What do I expect? What is this gift? The Spirit works in and through my human spirit. The Holy Spirit enlivens my spirit. Therefore I expect my spirit, i.e., my intellect, my feeling and will, to be stimulated by a spirit (the Holy Spirit) that awakens something that wasn't there before.

So when I am before God with an open mind and receive some original, fresh insight—is not that the Holy Spirit's gift? Such insight bestows a great comfort, renewed hope, special guidance for both the present moment and for long-range plans. These gifts might take the form of a word or a thought, an intuition or an impulse. It is important to grasp such impulses when they appear and not let them be crowded out by more mundane thoughts.

Spirit of God, make me open to your enlivening presence today!

A vocabulary for prayer

I need a vocabulary with which to think about God and with which I can talk with God. What kind of discourse is appropriate for a human being to talk with God? In a sense, the whole idea of such discourse is preposterous! Left to myself, I flounder for words that seem appropriate for talking with the Holy One.

But at this point the Bible gives me such a vocabulary. Through many diverse writings the Bible records such discourse of saints through the ages. It puts into words things that I feel vaguely in my heart. Thus the Bible is the best—though not the only—guide and "handbook" for finding appropriate subjects for prayer and words for prayer.

Worship the invisible God

The message of the Old Testament is clear in saying that the religious struggle of God's chosen people was to turn from visible forms of a deity ("idols") to the true, invisible God. This was the unique contribution of Israel to world religions, most of which worshipped some visible object. True, Buddhism tried, with dubious success, to be an exception to the worship of images, focusing, rather, on how to deal with the self.

And isn't this the struggle of modern people of faith as well—to experience the deity as a spiritual invisible reality rather than give top priority to a visible, secular entity such as money, house or entertainment, or to worship the invisible deity rather than give top priority to a religious entity such as a visible building or a ritual, or a book?" Top priority" is a synonym for "idol," and giving top priority to any of these things is indeed "idol worship." God help me to recognize the idols in my life and give them up for something more real.

Third Week   Monday   *God*

God in our consciousness

If God is a spirit and communicates with human beings, then does not God's spirit coincide with our spirit? The Holy Spirit is spirit. How can we distinguish between divine spirit and human spirit? Both are beyond explanation, beyond comprehension. To be close to God is to be highly aware of myself, my spirit. Any increase in consciousness of myself is an increase in spiritual capacity, an increase in the potential for God-likeness.

God, make me sensitive to my spirit, and to your Spirit!

Third Week   Tuesday   *Jesus Christ*

The shock of Christmas

Christmas is so much more than beauty, more than joy, more than something to sing praise about. Christmas is a shock!, an absolute surprise! Since the beginning of time no human being could ever have expected or predicted that God would manifest the divine Self to the world in this fashion! No one in the Judeo tradition of expecting a savior from God—the Messiah—ever imagined the Messiah would come in the form of a baby nestled on a bed of hay!

Is it any wonder that most of his contemporaries couldn't accept Jesus as Messiah! We must not lose this shocking aspect of Christmas.

Life, spirit and Spirit

More and more I am experiencing the unity of all life. The life in plants is amazing—the diversity and beauty of trees, flowers and fruit, the potential that lies dormant in seeds of all kinds. This manifestation of life is truly fantastic.

And there is the life of animals, with their power to be self-sustaining and mobile, to move at will for self-preservation. What amazing diversity and beauty in the birds, horses, dogs, fish, flies—and bacteria, without which we could not live! And all of the animals have this mind-boggling ability to reproduce their kind through a mysterious procreation process.

Then there is our human family, participating in so much that is common to the whole animal kingdom. But additionally, we have self-awareness or self-consciousness that we call spirit.

Finally, there is what Christians call the "Holy Spirit." Perhaps the Holy Spirit is a kind of process whereby the divine Spirit penetrates the human spirit and colors it with a quality of being different from the natural processes that sustain the various forms of life, a transforming quality like an unpredictable rush of surprising energy.

What a wonderful world! What a wonderful life!

Prayer, the essence of spirituality

Prayer is a profound, vital subject in religion. It is nothing less than the mode of human response to the divine presence. It is not just "saying prayers" in the sense of making petitions or praising God. It encompasses all of my feelings and concepts of how I relate to divine reality, and this is the very essence of spirituality. Learning to pray is a life-long task.

Light as a profound metaphor

The Bible frequently describes God and Jesus by using the metaphor of light. Why this metaphor? What are its implications? This word seems to make the divine nature extremely abstract and philosophical, while at the same time pointing to a meaning "as plain as day."

Light should be understood in contrast with darkness, its opposite. In the dark we get lost; we don't know the way. We can also hide what we're doing in the dark. In the light we can know where we're going, we can be aware of the way ahead, and we are exposed.

That is, in the light of Jesus' revelation of God we can know where life is leading us, what and where our destination is.

To walk in the light is to be open and honest with our behavior, not to hide in hypocrisy or cover-up, to be truthful about who we are and what we have done.

God, help me adventure into the Light!

"Father"

One of the great teachings and revelatory words left to us
by Jesus was his use of the word "Father" in speaking of
or to God. Jewish tradition talked of God as the awesome
Holy One. Religionists and philosophers through the ages,
and today, call God by innumerable names. But Jesus cut
through all the difficult abstractions people used to speak
of divinity and used this revolutionary little word, Father.
This word is startling in its simplicity and profundity.

I know there are objections to the "gender-specific" nature
of this word, and some would like to say "Mother" rather
than "Father." But in this case I want use the word that
Jesus used.

What does "father" mean to you?

This is good news

John ends his Gospel saying that the purpose of writing the Gospel is "that you may believe." The usual meaning of "believe" is to affirm (believe) that Jesus was the divine son of God. But what is there about that belief that constitutes the "good news" of the Gospel? What is there about such an affirmation that saves? How does simply an affirmation of belief give us new life?

Rather, isn't the meaning of "believe" something like this: Believe that God is like Jesus—one who loved all people unconditionally and healed diseases and fought patiently for the right. That our God is such a God is indeed good news! The Being who created and sustains us every minute of our lives is not a cold judge, not a distant machine, but One who loves unconditionally, who heals what is broken, who is always on the side of the right. "To believe" is to appropriate all this comfort and joy within ourselves.

Do you need a comforter?

Especially in John's Gospel there is much talk about the
coming of the *parakletos*, usually translated "Comforter."
This is his word for what we ordinarily call the "Holy
Spirit." This is a very significant and suggestive
appellation! A comforter is a warm and friendly presence
that embraces us and gives comfort in times of loneliness or
sorrow.

The Holy Spirit, translated "Holy Ghost" in former times,
is anything but a fearsome, ghostly being, but is, rather,
our constant Companion, our alter-ego, if you will, who is
always at our side.

Because of this wonderful primary relationship, we can
afford to lighten up on other relationships and attachments.
In fact, we are enabled to detach from whatever is
worthless or debilitating, and just cling to this Comforter
who is always there at our side responding to our needs.

How I need this Comforter today! Come, Holy Spirit!

Metaphors implicit in the Lord's Prayer

Consider the several significant metaphors for the nature of God, explicit or implicit, in the Lord's Prayer: father ("Our Father"), king ("Thy Kingdom come"), economist ("Give us daily bread"), mother (mother-like) ("Forgive us"), teacher ("Lead us not into temptation"), and finally, a transcendent sovereign ("Deliver us from evil"). Indeed this is a prayer full of "mixed metaphors"! But God is all of those things to us. No wonder it is hard—impossible—to visualize God as we pray.

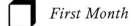

Can you discern the will of God?

What is that abstraction called the "will of God"? This phrase can be misused as a defense for shaky behavior, or as a slippery guide for the future.

But the will of God is that which is right for me and right for the world. I must keep my eyes on that right as though it is an anchor, a compass, a line that runs vertically up to and down from above, and then stretches out straight in front of me. This is the "plumb line" spoken of by the prophet Amos.

I align myself with this marker. When I am in an ambiguous situation, or a situation of anxiety, or when faced with a decision, I bring this image into awareness—a line running straight up and down. There is a "will" beyond me; it cuts right through me and challenges me to align myself with that sense of the right.

May thy will be done in my life today.

Second Month

San Diego scene

Watercolor, 2010

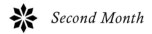

God is life

Who/what is God? Can we say it this way: God is the mystery we call "life"—human life, animal life, plant life—all life. Radical? Yes, but the phenomenon of life itself is also radically incomprehensible.

We believe in God's "incarnation" in Christ—God took on flesh. Can we extend that and acknowledge that, in one sense, God is incarnated—"enfleshed"—in all human life?

And is there reason to exclude other animal life, and plant life as well? Radical? Yes, but the phenomenon of all manifestations of what we call "life" is truly mysterious.

I pray that my eyes and heart will be open to the mystery of all life that surrounds me.

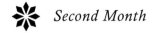

First Week   *Tuesday*   *Who was Jesus?*

Jesus as *logos*

John's Gospel avoids historical difficulties with Jesus'
birth by putting Jesus in a supra-historical setting—"the
eternal logos made flesh." This is a philosophical approach
to understanding Jesus. It stands in contrast to the Gospel
according to Matthew, who puts him very much into the
context of Jewish history by recording his genealogy, and
also in contrast to Luke, who not only surrounds Jesus'
birth with stories of a manger and shepherds, but precedes
the birth with the story of his forerunner, John the Baptist,
another bold historical figure.

The logos, or divine expression, that created the world is
the logos that manifests itself in Jesus. In that light St. Paul
can say, "All things were created through Christ." As logos
we can perceive the "cosmic Christ" in every aspect of the
created world, including nature—even today.

God, open my eyes that I may see the divine expression in
all things around me.

Word of God, word of man

Christians claim that the Bible is the very Word of God, but also a human word. These two are not easily reconciled. But they can be understood on this premise: God spoke his living word to people who lived in a certain historical and cultural context, and they understood that Word in a way that was relevant to their situation. Over a period of some 3000 years the cultural context has dramatically changed, so the words of divine guidance will need to change in accordance with changing human perception arising from changing cultures.

This way of thinking does not allow us to hold the words of any book as absolute and ultimate. It does allow us to see that the Word has a human character, because it is known only through revelations of the divine to certain people who lived in certain times and had certain ways of perceiving and expressing themselves. The only way God speaks is through people; therefore, there need be no discrepancy between the Word of God and the human words as we find these in the Bible. God, what is your word to me today?

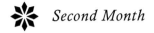

God's work, my work

There is profound truth beneath the old adage, When you pray, pray as if all depends on God; when you work, work as if all depends on you.

   Everything depends on God, yet God's way of working is through my work. If I'm not functioning at my best, neither is the divine power functioning at its best. The pious prayer, "Lord, please help me do...." can be invalidated by my own lack of participation or laziness. I want to cooperate with the divine plan today.

First Week   *Friday*   *Reflections*

Just "to be"

To be—this is my task. Not to wait for a better day, not to worry about the future or feel guilt for the past, but just to be what I am now, before God, who knows me completely. Not to be self-conscious around others, wondering what they're thinking of me, not to worry about how to "act" around others, but just to be myself—communicating what is necessary when and to whom it is necessary. Beyond that, I just try to keep silent and be content to listen, or just be present—this is the stance I desire now. God help me just to be!

Second Week   *Monday*   *Nature of God*

God is personal

Christianity holds to the existence of a personal God. If I am a Christian, I do not necessarily believe that God is a person, but I do believe God must be personal, fine as that distinction may seem. We believe this because we hold Jesus Christ to be the historical center of our faith, and Jesus believed in a personal God, for he prayed, "Our Father who art in heaven," and called upon "my Father who is in heaven."

This is a distinctive point of view of the Christian faith, and sets it apart from the almost universal belief in some "Higher Power."

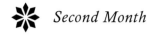

Second Week   Tuesday *Jesus Christ*

Transcending time and space

Here is a thought for our celebration of Easter. The resurrection event was a must in God's revelation of the divine self to the world. For what more distinguishing characteristic of God is there than God's transcendence of time and space?

Our death as human beings is the starkest reminder of our human time-space limitation. There is an end to our time on earth; there is an end to this physical body which occupies space.

But the resurrection of Jesus Christ proclaims that God transcends time and space; that's what makes God truly Other. If God wanted to reveal the divine Otherness to the human race, how better to do that than through a mighty act that would demonstrate the overcoming of death—the symbol of time and space. So the Christ, revealing the divine nature, was necessarily raised from the dead.

O God, if you can even overcome time and space, why should I doubt that you can overcome the minor obstacles in my life that I face today.

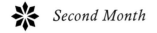

Second Week   Wednesday   *The Spirit*

Spirit—natural or super-natural?

It is increasingly obvious to our generation of therapists, mind trainers, New Age practitioners, those who meditate, "faith healers," etc., that unseen spiritual energy is indeed available to us. It seems to be simply a part of the nature of things. This spiritual energy, although it defies the usual categories of scientific measurement, is a part of the world given us to explore and utilize.

Whether or not we call it "super-natural" may be a moot question, because this spiritual energy seems to be an integral part of the universal human potential, rather than a super-natural phenomenon.

My concern is how to relate this human spirit to the spirit of the Almighty, which we call the "Holy Spirit." This is an ongoing quest. May the Holy Spirit touch me this day and breathe vigor and hope into my spirit!

Second Week   Thursday   *The Way*

The *agape* force

Love and creativity, the two cornerstones of my philosophy of life, are both products of the *agape* (outgoing love) force. That is, they both are outward movements, energy flowing out from, not into myself. Finding ways and means of caring for others, focusing on ideas and activities outside myself, working on projects outside myself—these are paths that express both love and creativity. I hope I can be creatively loving and lovingly creative today.

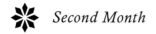

Libido, eros, philia

Tillich analyzed love by saying that all love is characterized by three qualities—libido, eros and philia. According to him libido plays a primary role in every act of relatedness, because it is the organic or physiological foundation of loving relationships. Thus a frustration of libido would mean a frustration throughout all loving relationships.

But I argue with this. Is not relatedness built on other foundations, such as creativity, power, enjoyment, etc.? The three qualities should be considered separately. Libido is a glandular mechanism that can be satisfied in a number of ways, and is not necessarily connected with eros and philia. Eros can be satisfied by the sheer appreciation of beauty. Philia can be satisfied by social commonality of interests, work and play.

Indeed, love is a many-splendored thing!

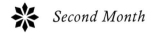

Third Week   Monday   *Nature of God*

The divine bubbles up into history

I tend to think of God in philosophical and universal terms. Then I participate in the Holy Communion—eat bread and drink wine and hear those words, "This is my body...this is my blood." That act is utterly specific, historical, material, particular. This eating and drinking has been observed in Christianity for 2000 years. We remember and receive the God-man Jesus.

In this Eucharist we experience how there is an occasional revelation of the divine spilling out into history. There is a bubbling up of the divine into the human world like bubbles that rise to the surface of a slow cooking pot. The whole pot doesn't explode into gas all at once, but here and there is a tiny explosion of liquid into gas—what a transformation! Then the air bubbles come to the surface where they can be seen and observed.

Just as an energy source—heat—necessarily lies behind the transformation into bubbles, so there has to be an unseen but real "Energy Source"—unseen but real— giving rise to the "bubbles" of certain unexplainable phenomena.

Let's be alert today for any divine "bubbling" occurring in our environment.

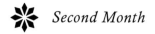

Third Week   *Tuesday*   *Who was Jesus*

The cross as a sacrament

The Cross event should not be seen as Jesus offering a sacrifice to please, much less appease God, as some interpret the Cross. For if God was truly in Jesus the Christ, then it was God suffering on the Cross with mankind. God was suffering for us, not the man Jesus offering something to appease an angry God.

The Cross event is, rather, a sacramental act, sacrament being defined as an expression of divine grace in human action.

Thank you, Lord, for the amazing grace shown to us in the Cross event!

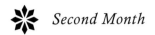

"Do this in remembrance of me"

In the Eucharist liturgy we recite the "Words of Institution:" "This is my body given for you; do this in remembrance of me." Perhaps the last half of this sentence should be taken to mean, "To do something in remembrance of me, go do what I am doing—giving myself sacrificially to carry out my mission in the world."

What was his mission? Perhaps these words refer to both the actual way Jesus lived out his life and ministry, and his final culmination of sacrifice for others, which St. Paul and others interpreted according to the Jewish system of ritual sacrifice. It was both the climax of a life lived out in obedience to the Father and a once-and-for all sacrifice. Thus these words can simultaneously be a gracious gift and a call to mission.

Lutherans are so concerned about "consubstantiation" in the Eucharist as over against the Reformed Church's accent on "remembrance" that they tend to overlook the reality of Jesus' word, "Remember me."

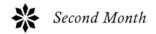

Third Week   *Thursday*   *Lord's Prayer*

"Hallowed be thy name"

"Hallowed be thy name," the first petition of the Lord's Prayer is perhaps the most appropriate prayer we can offer. We often pray, Be with me—but God is always with us. We pray, God help us—but God is always working for us. We pray, Give us your grace—but God's grace is always surrounding us. We pray, Be near me—but God is already nearer than my breath.

So let us just be quiet and say, "Great and glorious God, I honor your name; I honor you above everything else; I bow before your awesome Being; make this a hallowed moment. I wait upon you now."

Third Week   *Friday*   *Reflections*

The meaning of my life

What then is the meaning of my life? For starters, I can share the following statements: The meaning of my life is to know that I am in harmony with the God who sustains my life; to know Jesus Christ who was and is the key to fulfilled humanity; to be with and work with people on worthy projects; to understand people's anguish and help them attain peace; to enjoy and strengthen the ties among my family; to discover and share a theology which has relevance for people's everyday life; to enjoy and express myself through the arts, and to cultivate a sound body.

These give me ample reasons for living. What motivates you to get going every morning?

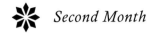

Fourth Week   Monday   *Nature of God*

God pours out love

The essence of Christian faith is recognizing God as a
loving God. What manner of existence God has, what
concepts we use to define or describe God—all this is
very secondary to the recognition that this divine entity
is characterized by an outpouring that we call love. The
whole creation, including my own self, lies in the caress
of that outpouring of love. This is a love that cares for the
creation, that calls all things to grow and develop, that
accepts us human beings as we are and coaxes us into a
better tomorrow. This is the doctrine of grace; this is the
meaning of "God so loved the world…." Thank you God!

Fourth Week   Tuesday   *The Cross event*

Jesus' death as sacrifice

The death of Jesus was simultaneously a fulfillment of the
old Covenant between God and Israel and the initiation of
a new Covenant. That is, one act was at once a sacrifice that
fulfilled the demand given to the Jewish people for a "sin
offering" to God, but it was absolutely new in that it was an
act of self-sacrifice in order to fulfill a mission.

Substitutionary atonement theory to the contrary,
I believe it was not a ritual death offering blood for
atonement as the people of Israel had been compelled to do
throughout the centuries, but the sacrifice of an entire life to
carry out a God-given ministry. And in the act of carrying
out that ministry to the full, Jesus got killed. A sacrifice—
yes indeed!

When I think of Christ's sacrifice for the world, including
me, I'm ashamed that I sacrifice so little for him.

Fourth Week   *Wednesday*   *Sacrament*

Uniqueness of the Eucharist

Does any other religion have anything like the Eucharist (or Holy Communion) in its rituals? For other religions, religion means a certain way of thinking and believing or acting or beseeching God/gods for blessings. The Christian Eucharist is different. It is the celebration of a historical person and a historical event. It is not just a teaching, but an activity, an event that reenacts the primal historical event of Jesus' life and death and resurrection. This is a pivotal event for Christians. It epitomizes the whole of Christianity: God in the world, acting for us, in history, and today.

What a privilege to participate in this event!

Fourth Week   *Thursday*   *The Lord's Prayer*

The meaning of "to hallow"

This phrase, Hallowed be thy name, is grammatically strange. It is not an active voice that says, "May I hallow your name," but instead says, "God, make yourself holy among us." And that is a difficult concept for us to wrap our minds around! Does it imply something like this: "Let us experience the halo of your mystic presence in the mundane affairs of life. Material things are too much with us, they have too strong a hold on us. Give us an experience of a quiet Otherness in the midst of all this worldly stuff and noisy secular life."

As we begin to pray, these words nudge us, saying, "Remember the Holy One is here."

What is your life orientation?

Many of us have been trained to be "person-oriented" and "being-oriented" in our outlook on life. Important as that perspective is, there comes a time when we realize the need to move toward being more "doing-oriented" or "task-oriented."

We say we are members of the Kingdom of God. The Kingdom of God is a place to work and serve; it is something to build up. For myself, "What is the work I should be doing?" has become a more important question than, "Is my inner life fulfilled and happy?"

This perspective is especially applicable to us when we are in our middle years. When we reach the later years of life, the "doing" often becomes physically impossible, and then it is important to shift back to "being." Both should be in a proper balance throughout our lifetime.

Third Month

Flight of fantasy

Watercolor, 2010

First Week *Monday* *God*

"I believe in…the Maker"

"I believe in God the Father Almighty, Maker of Heaven and Earth." When I perceive in my inner sense as well as with my external senses the miracle of the natural universe, including the human self, my only worthy response is these beginning words of the first article of the Apostles' Creed. And they are similar in intent to the beginning words of the Lord's Prayer, "Our Father in heaven, hallowed be your name." These two statements are the foundation of my faith.

First Week *Tuesday* *Jesus Christ*

Christ brings God into a human body

What words are more bandied about in Christendom than, "Believe in Christ—and be saved." But what does that really mean anyway? What kind of a person was this Jesus in whom we are to believe?

Jesus saw himself as the one who was completely open and translucent before God, the one through whom God was at work in the world. So to "believe in Jesus" is to believe that God actually is a living, loving Being who is not separated from this world, but who is really living among us, breaking into our human drama. God is a God who can be "incarnated," i.e., who can bring the divine into a human body, yes, into human bodies, like yours and mine.

Birth, death and eternal life

"Eternal life"—a central theme of Jesus according to the Gospel of John—is nothing other than the end of the whole birth-death cycle of all nature, either in terms of a new kind of existence beyond that cycle, or a completely new dimension to that cycle.

But do I really believe in that "eternal life"? Do I hope for eternal life myself? James Cone, in an interview with Bill Moyers, focused on the theme of hope. Anything that gave Blacks hope in the midst of their suffering was their salvation throughout their history. To have hope in the midst of suffering, and to affirm a life beyond the birth-death cycle are analogous; they are both acts of faith.

We just have to take a plunge—either we believe there is another stage of existence different from this one, or we don't. "Believing" is more than intellectual assent, but the element of intellectual assent is also important. I can say, "Yes, I believe there is Something More, and so I live in hope," or I can say, "No, I can't believe there is Something More," and end up in hopelessness.

God, give me faith and hope in the midst of uncertainty.

What to say in prayer

When you stop to think about it, prayer is a very bold, yes, presumptuous act—I, a little grain of dust pretending to communicate with the One who created and upholds the universe! What kind of nonsense is that! So if I pray, what should I say, what kind of words might be acceptable? I surely am not in a position to make demands and petty requests of God. And God certainly does not need my little thank-yous for the good things in life.

But the prayer that Jesus taught gives us a clue about what to say: Begin with "Hallowed be thy name." Here is the appropriate starting point. To hallow the name of God, i.e., to acknowledge and hold in respect and reverence the mystery of the Maker of heaven and earth, the eternal Holy One. I believe this is an appropriate starting place as we attempt to offer a prayer.

My four pillars

My philosophy of life has boiled down to these four elements:

1) Awareness: insofar as possible, being constantly aware of the who, what, where, when, how, why of every moment. Being aware makes me different from the lower animals.

2) Gratitude: constantly being grateful and giving thanks to God and those around us for the blessing of being alive in a wonderful, abundant universe.

3) Creativity: working to make something useful or beautiful, doing something constructive for the direct or indirect benefit of others.

4) Love: putting the welfare of others and the world ahead of my own self-seeking interests, knowing there is always someone who needs my creative service.

God cannot be hurt!

If God is truly the ineffable "All in all," then God is reality itself, truth itself. No amount of questioning on my part can hurt such a One. If our religious faith is focused on this true God, then we are free to ask questions of traditional doctrine and the Bible and worship practice. Surely God wants honesty rather than orthodoxy. For truth can stand on its own feet without the props of piety or any certain traditional beliefs. The only word that can hurt God is "No thank you."

Feel free to raise questions!

"My body given for you"

As Jesus' final words to his disciples at the Last Supper he said, "This is my body given for you." "My body" can be understood to refer to his entire bodily life—not just the body that would be hanging on a cross, but all he had been and done and taught and suffered—all was "for you." He was not under compulsion to do this. He gave us his earthly life out of love for the human race.

Thus we can say that he died for us, but we should never forget that he also lived his whole life for us. This love overwhelms me!

Hallowing the name, acknowledging the reign

Many people in various religious traditions around the world hallow the name of God, or their god, in some form or another.

But not as many recognize that the God whom they reverence has a "Kingdom" and rules the world according to the divine will, as the Lord's Prayer indicates to us. The Christian understanding of God cannot stop with worshiping the sacred name, but must immediately follow worship with a recognition of the authority of God over our everyday behavior: "Thy Kingdom come; thy will be done."

Integrity

Integrity is being honest to God. It is laying my whole mind and will open before God, and asking God to lead the way. When I do this, relations with others also become more open and honest. As a result, life becomes more unified and wholesome.

The opposite is to live in defensive self-deception, not being open and honest with either myself or with God. If I live this way, I have no power because I am divided, torn and frustrated. Energies are used up trying to hide from or run away from some area of darkness.

This kind of open integrity is spelled out in Jesus' words, "He who does evil hates the truth, because it exposes his deeds. He who does right loves the truth because it exposes his deeds as being right." (John 3)

It's difficult to dive in

My constant temptation is to walk around the pool, seeing it as a beautiful body of water, ruminating about the nice feel of the water, but never diving in. Why do we hesitate so often to take the dive, to immerse ourselves, allow the water to buoy us up, to feel the joy of total immersion? Mere cogitation and rationality are such poor substitutes for the real thing.

Thinking about the pool is theology; diving into the pool is faith. There is a vast difference between talking about God and talking to God. The former is the stance of the theologian; the latter is the stance of the person of faith. These two are not necessarily the same. The first is an academic exercise; the latter is an existential experience. The former calls for intellect; the latter calls for courage. God, give me the courage to take the plunge today!

God walks our dusty path

Let us think of the whole universe as being God's body, God's face as all human faces. The more I know about my body and about nature, the more I know and appreciate God, because that is where God is. God does not sit on a landing dock up in outer space. Likewise, the more I understand about the human spiritual constitution, both my own and others, the more I know and appreciate the divine Spirit. The Spirit is not flying around like angels in a Christmas scene. The Spirit of God is walking with you and me on today's dusty path.

The fountain of forgiveness

"Father, forgive them for they know not what they do."
These were not simply momentary words that happened to
cross Jesus' lips at his last moment on the cross. Rather, they
reflect the essence of Jesus' whole life. He did not condemn.
Even in the Passion event he was silent before his torturers;
he did not blurt out anger or revenge on sinners.

However, if we look at the greed and jealousy and hatred
that sent Jesus finally to his crucifixion, we see how much
damage sin does, how much suffering it causes. In that light
the crucifixion of the Son of God can be seen as a historical
display of God taking the consequences of sin into God's
own self, and then saying, "Father, forgive them."

Thus we can say that Christ's death is vicarious, because
in the Cross event he was suffering in a way that all
humanity should have been suffering. This vicarious act is
the fountain of divine forgiveness.

Third Week   *Wednesday*   *Commitment*

Another daily miracle

A miracle happened again today. Yesterday was a time of pressure and anxiety and inner confusion. But this morning I started the day with silence, inner assessment, confession of my true feelings and anxieties, and then turned everything over to the power of the Spirit, to the working of grace. I asked for nothing, but simply entrusted myself and the day into the hands of the One who cares infinitely for us.

That One said, "My grace is sufficient for you. Have a good day!" And indeed it has been a good day! There were challenges, but everything went calmly and smoothly, with joy filling in the cracks.

Thank God, this gracious work of the Spirit occurs often enough to keep my faith alive, to make me know that God is, and is an active force in the world!

Third Week   *Thursday*   *The Way*

Live proactively!

There are two basically different ways for human living from day to day. One way is the "natural" way, just letting nature take its course, being prompted to act by what is seen and heard and felt from the stimuli in our environment. We live moment to moment, reacting to circumstances.

The other way is to live proactively, with guidance from an inner voice that lures us in creative directions and gives us long-range goals. We can live being constantly aware of an overlay, or an undergirding, of a spiritual layer of our life in which the divine presence is working.

This presence doesn't meet the senses, but is nonetheless very real. This presence is like light, which is nothing in itself, but the presence or absence of which makes all the difference. It spurs us on toward a proactive stance in the world, acting creatively rather than simply responding to stimuli.

Third Week   *Friday*   *The Way*

God's way, the right way

We pray for the Kingdom of God to come and the will of God to be done. What is the will of God? What is the ethical principle in the will of God? Stated most simply, is it not the right way for human life to be lived? Doing things as they ought to be done according to original intent?

In some cases the right way is obvious, but in other cases it must be determined by intensive study of history and sociology and psychology, and in consultation with others.

O God, life is difficult and complex. Show us the right way, and the courage to follow that way.

Fourth Week   *Monday*   *God*

The invisible God

The invisible God was the God Israel was called to
worship, even though they were constantly tempted to
substitute a visible for the invisible god. That is no wonder.
Worshipping and trusting an unseen God has seemed
foolish to all people through all ages, as it does to me
sometimes. Yet this is the essence of the Judeo-Christian
God—the object of our worship is invisible. This truth gives
birth to trouble for the rational mind, but also gives birth to
awe and wonder for the seeking soul.

Absolutely no thing can be revered as God. I.e., the whole
O.T. teaching about God was first of all to abstain from
worshiping idols—things. But if we conceive of God as "
a Being" similar to our human image, is this not also
creating a kind of idol, for "a Being" presents us with an
image of a thing like other beings are things. In Jewish-
Christian thought, the essence of the divine is that the
divine is the unseen Mystery of the universe.

God's biggest surprise

During Jesus' final trial, Pilate asked him, "Are you the Son of God?" Jesus does not deny it. "What more evidence against him do we need? He says he is the Son of God." His interrogators knew that this must be a lie, a blasphemy. A key motivation for killing Jesus was simply that human beings could not tolerate the idea of God appearing in the form of an ordinary low class person.

I.e., Jesus was the kind of person so far removed from their expectation of the Messiah, that to them this man saying he was the Messiah or Son of God had to be an absurd lie. This kind of divine revelation was utterly foreign to both the Jews and the Roman authorities of the day. So they got rid of the imposter, which they thought was the only proper thing to do.

How about us? Is God showing himself in ways we cannot fathom, in ways that run utterly counter to our expectations? Is God appearing in some lowly form that we completely fail to recognize?

Let us walk in the light

It is the duty of all human beings to walk in the light they have been granted. It is the privilege of some of us to know Jesus Christ and walk in his light.

Those two sentences express my growing view of the relationship of Christianity and other religions. Those of us who know the Christian Gospel have the very great privilege and responsibility of walking in a bright light. Those who do not know the Christian Gospel also have received light. A just and righteous God will surely judge humanity by how each of us has followed the light given us, or to use a biblical metaphor, how well we have used the talent entrusted to us.

Another thought follows: those of us who know the value of the bright light will also be judged on how well we share that valuable asset with people straining to see in their dimmer light.

What am I doing with "this little light of mine"?

In harmony with the universe

To be in harmony with the world of sun, moon and stars,
the world of trees, grass and flowers, the world of horses,
birds and pet dogs as well as the world of people—
is not this the end of all religion? To many believers this
may seem materialistic, humanistic, almost pantheistic.
However, just to be what the Creator intended me to be,
to care for the wonderful world that surrounds me—isn't
this living for God, and also fulfilling my own God-given
potential? We are saved by grace, and it is indeed grace
that I experience filling the whole world around me. It is
enough just to sink into that grace and give thanks.

Religious experience and esthetic experience

For me these two are closely linked. My esthetic sense—
the appreciation of beauty—is part of my spirituality.
I am not talking about the objective things that we might
call beautiful, but about the inner sense or sensibility that
something which impinges on one or more of my senses
produces a profound experience of pleasure.

Two people can look at the same picture, or face, or
mountain scene and describe it objectively with similar
words; however, the esthetic experience, the intangible
quality of pleasure might be quite different for each of
them.

The esthetic experience overlaps with religious experience
when it issues in joy, awe, and praise to the Giver of all
good gifts.

Fourth Month

Probing unknown spaces

Oil, 2010

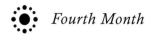

First Week   *Monday*   *God*

Always a seeker

The Psalmist continually speaks of "seeking God." This is
a very significant expression. It is perhaps the best stance
for anyone to take—non-Christian layman or Christian
theologian! It has two edges: 1) We can never discover God
completely, never "catch" God. God forever eludes human
understanding, so we must continue to seek God.

2) However, seeking also implies an active stance. It is not
just vaguely longing for God; it is the work of searching. I
ask myself daily, am I truly seeking God with all my heart?

First Week   *Tuesday*   *Jesus Christ*

Praying in a lonely place

There is frequent reference in the Gospels to Jesus going
to a lonely place to pray. It is interesting that there is no
mention of going to the temple to pray. He might well have
done so, but there is no specific reference to that. This leads
us to think that Jesus was more a private mystic than a
public worshiper.

This is also a model for us. "Doing the liturgy" in church
on Sunday morning is not enough. There should at least be
a "both-and" for private meditation and public worship.

We need an objective anchor

Without the Bible, our spiritual life is nebulous, wandering, unfocused, prone to all kinds of deviation. The Bible is an objective thing, an objective written word. It is something to latch on to which has stabilizing power, an anchor.

It is a public document that everyone can use, and thus it should (but does not always) unite the Christian family. Without it we swim aimlessly in subjectivity, in whirlpools of introspection which offer no ultimate goals or guidance toward those goals.

I am not a "fundamentalist," but I thank God daily for the light that comes into my life through the Scriptures, and I hold the Bible as the most valuable book in my library

---

I am part of the whole

As I looked with awe at the vast cloud formations in a deep blue sky this morning, it came as a joyful insight that this sky is not a separate object from the earth, and it is not separate from me, a product of the earth. I am a part of the vast whole! I am an integral part, one piece with the great universe. I belong to it and it belongs to me. The Creator has put me here to care for the creation. What a vocation!

Continual turning

We need to be in a state of continual repentance, which means "turning around," because our natural tendency is always to turn inward and follow whatever physical or emotional impulse is there. But this action becomes a downward spiral.

The challenge is to be aware of this natural tendency and continually turn outward and upward, looking expectantly to the Higher Power for hope and guidance. In this daily attitude of "repentance" lies challenge and fulfillment.

Grant me the courage to turn around and face heaven-ward today!

Second Week   Monday   *God*

For the praise of the Creator

When I consider the awesome majesty and intricate
marvels of nature—the volcanoes, the flowers, the quarks,
the procreation process—I cannot help but ask, "For what
purpose does this wonderful universe exist?" The answer
comes, "For the praise of the Creator."

So what is our place in this great scheme of things? The
place of us human beings, bestowed with the high gift
of consciousness and intelligence and freedom, must be
simply to give praise to the Creator, to hallow the holy
name of the Creator of heaven and earth.

Lord, make me aware of this high calling today!!

Second Week   Tuesday   *Who was Jesus?*

The greater reality is God

C. K. Barrett, an authority on John's Gospel, says "For
John the historical figure of Jesus was central for his
understanding of God; central, but not final....There could
hardly be a more Christocentric writer than John, yet his
very Christocentricity is theocentric."

In simpler language, Barrett is saying that although Jesus
Christ is central in this Gospel, he is always subjugated
under the greater reality of the invisible, eternal God. I
have always felt this about the Gospel according to St. John,
where a key word is "Not I, but the Father...." Contrary
to parts of the worship liturgy—e.g., the Te Deum—the
ultimate object of Christian worship is God, not Jesus.

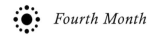

Second Week   Wednesday   *Sacrament*

Sacrament and Incarnation

The sacrament of the Holy Communion as observed in
our churches proclaims to us that God is in this physical
world in two dimensions: in the person of Jesus, and in the
Sacrament, both of which proclaim incarnation.

This is the significant point of the Sacrament: God is not
separate from our material life. God is in the world. God
continually reveals the divine Self in human ways.

It is my experience that this meaning is slighted in the
Lutheran service of Holy Communion, which is focused
mainly on receiving forgiveness of sin, which is a part, but
only a part of the drama of the Eucharist.

Second Week   Thursday   *Prayer*

How to pray intercessory prayer

The focus of my prayer for others must be on the other
person and on God, not on the adequacy of my own
intercession.

Focusing on the other broadens my horizon, broadens
my caring, and broadens the scope of my love. Focusing
on God recognizes that it is not I who am doing something
for the person for whom I pray, but God, who can do much
more for that person than I can imagine.

May God grant that even my inadequate prayers for my
friends might open a faucet for divine power to pour out.

Dealing with weakness

The challenge to every person is how to deal with our weaknesses. Some of the possible ways include:

1) Overcoming the weakness and eliminating it. Usually we think only of this approach, it is the heroic way;

2) Living around the weakness, while it still remains; being resigned to coping rather than overcoming

3) Playing a game with the weakness, taking it with a touch of humor, not succumbing to it but finding creative ways to interact with it.

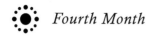

Third Week   *Monday*   *The Nature of God*

Confronting traditional concepts

If it is legitimate to believe that God is in everything, in
me, and in the universe as his "body," as some theologians
say, then how does that affect traditional concepts such as:
God created the world; God sent his Son down to earth;
Jesus ascended up to the right hand of the Father; we die
and go to heaven to be with God, and so forth? We need
to be humble and open our minds to entirely new ways of
thinking about God and God in the world.

The clash of two forces

If pan-entheism (God in everything) is the best concept to use in thinking about God (as the Process theologians tell us), and if we say "God is love," then we can see all the power of life as somehow being the power of love. Love is like a centrifugal force—always thrusting us outward.

But there is an opposing force—centripetal force, the force of gravity—always pulling things inward toward the self. This is the natural pull toward self-preservation, so powerful in all human beings.

These two forces inevitably collide. If God were to be manifest in a historical human person there would inevitably be a deadly clash. Jesus sensed this from the beginning; therefore his premonitions or "predictions" of his death. Ordinary people, and not least the leaders of religion and politics, were controlled by the centripetal force—desiring only their own power and prestige, whereas Jesus was totally "centrifugal."

So how did Jesus see God's plan for him? He had two choices: to show ultimate victory through conquest by force, or to let his true nature—love for God and humanity—manifest itself to the full. Since the other Force could not tolerate that, it issued in an inevitable clash. But Jesus was willing to engage in the clash, even knowing it would mean sacrificing his very life. Jesus therefore had to be a sacrifice—a sacrifice that proved the character of love.

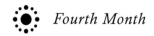

Baptism as covenant

Too often the baptism of infants seems to be a churchly ritual and nothing more. But if we think of baptism as the covenant which God makes with individuals as they start out their life, baptism does have deep meaning. The concept of covenant is simply the assurance that the nature and promise of God is to be gracious, beneficial, loving and forgiving to this child throughout his/her life, as to all humankind.

Of course, it is also essential that the parents provide an environment in which this covenant can be appreciated and "fleshed out" as the child grows older.

Third Week   *Thursday*   *Prayer*

A daily prayer for busy people

O God of grace and glory, may I be aware of your presence today.

Give me a heart to love you, to love your people, to love your earth.

Guide all I think and do and say today.

And make me grateful for all that is past, and for all that will be today. Amen.

Third Week   *Friday*   *Reflections*

Our policy of fear

Our current national policy is based on fear—fear of the terrorists. So our top priority becomes protecting ourselves through military action killing the terrorists. But seeing their cohorts killed is a major motivation for more and more Middle Eastern people to join the terrorists.

I think that the greatest challenge to both the military and diplomatic corps is to create strategies that would undercut the motivation of terrorists and their terrible actions and turn them into contented world citizens. Simplistic? Of course! But can you disagree with the principle?

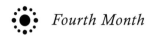

Can evolution account for gravity?

Many modern people see no need for God because evolutionary theory answers all the questions about the beginning of life and its many miracles. OK; let that stand. But evolutionary theory is not helpful if we ask a prior question: Why is there the phenomenon of gravity in the universe? Or why is there the phenomenon of electro-magnetism? Without the amazing balance of these forces in "nature" there would be no world as we know it. The earth and sun and stars would not exist. So where shall we go to answer those questions, unless it be to the Mystery that lies far beyond, behind, under, above evolutionary theory.

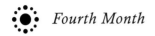

The clash of two forces (continued from previous week)

To be true to his mission, Jesus had to sacrifice himself, had to become a "sacrificial lamb." But this sacrificial lamb was not like the sacrificial lambs of the old covenant between God and his chosen people Israel. Rather, it was an entirely new way of thinking, a new spiritual structure, a "New Covenant."

Since God could not ultimately suffer defeat at the hands of the Centripetal (self-seeking) Power, there had to be a way, a surprise ending never before dreamed of in human history—the resurrection from the dead. The worldly powers used all the force they could against him, used their final climactic weapon—death, but even that did not overcome Jesus; he overcame it.

Even now this resurrected Centrifugal Power (love reaching out) still works redemptively in the world. This is the Spirit of the Living Christ, working to help and heal and bring all people to the knowledge of the divine victory, the "Centrifugal Way." This is the way of loving the unlovely. This is the way of the Cross.

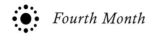
The contemporary Word of God

The concept of "Word of God" is absolutely basic for
Christian thought. But what does it refer to? Surely not
just to the Bible. It refers to the Bible only in the sense that
the Bible is a recording of messages believed to be divine
by persons who lived at various times in various places.
"Word of God" is a communication from God, a touching of
earth by the heavens. It is the still, small voice that whispers
to the human conscience.

And this God is still speaking! If God is truly a living
God, there is no reason not to believe that God is speaking
contemporary messages and doing new things in our
day. God has been doing new things every day since the
beginning of creation! While it is important to study the
meaning of the words recorded in the Bible, it is equally
important to listen to what the Spirit is saying today.

Fourth Week   *Thursday*   *The Way*

Remember the entire human family

In the Lord's Prayer we pray, "Thy Kingdom come."
Why did Jesus use the term "Kingdom" here and in many
parables? Some people these days object to this word
because of its connotations of male dominance, but it is
one of many metaphors for the reign of God in the world.
It would be impossible to eliminate this word from biblical
language.

"Kingdom" is a big word; it connotes a large entity.
Metaphorically, God is the King, and God reigns over the
entire human race, the whole earth, the entire universe.
God's reign includes nature and human society as well as
the individual heart.

Therefore, if we claim to be subjects of God's Kingdom,
we must have a broad view of life and define "the good"
in terms of what is good for the entire human family, for
the whole earth.

Fourth Week   *Friday*   *Reflections*

"In the eye of the beholder"

There is no objective thing that we can call "beauty."
The history of the arts gives ample evidence of this.
There are sounds, colors, forms which are the ingredients,
but beauty lies in the eye of the beholder, i.e., in the
perception and awareness of something that provokes a
certain spiritual excitement. I am thankful to God for this
awareness that responds to sound, color and form in such a
way that I can experience the joy of beauty.

Fifth Month

Division

Oil, 2009

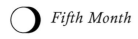

What makes God God?

I know that God is in my individual awareness, in my spirit. I have many experiences that testify to this. And if God is in me, then God must be in all human beings, and not only now, but in all human beings from the beginning of time to the end of time. But this universal immanence completely defies human comprehension.

I also know God is somehow present in the vast energies of the universe, in the billions of suns in our galaxy, and in the billions of galaxies, each with billions of suns, each sun millions of miles separated from each other. But this universal immanence defies our comprehension.

In this lies the "impossibility of God," which is the mystery of God, beyond all comprehension. If I can comprehend God, that God would no longer be God. The very ludicrousness of the existence of a God who is both in my consciousness in this moment, and who fills the unfathomable universe—this is what makes God God!

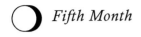

Forgiveness through the cross—how?

We say God forgives us for Jesus' sake, forgives because of
the cross. The old substitutionary atonement theory first
created by Anselm in the twelfth century comes to mind.
But there are many ways of looking at what the whole Cross
event means.

   Here is one way: If God is like Jesus and if Jesus said
to his killers, "Father, forgive them," then we know God
is indeed a forgiving God. So we can say that Jesus' last
words on the cross were the final demonstration of a
forgiving God interacting with sinners. We believe God still
interacts in that way with us.

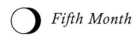

The Bible is a cradle

Martin Luther likened the Bible to the cradle that held the Christ-child. That is, it is a humble vessel or "container." We see both Jesus and the Bible as the Word of God, and the Incarnation principle says that the Word of God is both divine and human. That is, they both have their human, earthly, physical, contextual, historical aspect; the divine message is incarnated in this material context. Both are fully human and fully divine. Fully human means Jesus' body was frail; it means the book called the Bible is frail. Fully divine means Jesus' message brought us God's truth and grace; it means the book called the Bible brings us God's truth and grace.

This day also, we live in that mystical mix of the frail and the powerful, of the human and the divine.

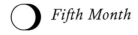

The all-inclusive Lord's Prayer

The Lord's Prayer is a prayer for the community and the world, not just for me. Its petitions have the widest possible scope of meaning. It is a statement that gives us big, broad strokes, in sparse language, which cover the whole of Christian thought and life. Consider the implications of the seven petitions of that prayer.

1) "Hallowed be thy name" Recognition of and reverence for the existence of the Holy One. 2) "Thy Kingdom come" Recognition that all things in heaven and earth are subject to this Holy One. 3) "Thy will be done" There is a right and wrong way for the human family to live, but God has a will and a way that we will do well to heed.

4) "Give us this day our daily bread." This God is concerned about our physical life, so one of our primary tasks is to satisfy needs, not just my own, but the needs of the whole human race. 5) "Forgive us our sins as we forgive those who sin against us." The rule of ethical living is to be humble enough to recognize that I am not, and no one else is, perfect; therefore we stand in constant need of forgiveness and must be tolerant and forgiving of one another in order to live together in community. 6) "Lead us not into temptation." There is a force pulling us away from the will of God, from the good; this is temptation, and we need divine help to stay on track.

7) "Deliver us from evil." The human family hopes for a final, blessed consummation when evil will be completely abolished.

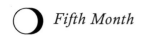

Living with ambiguity

I think we must be willing to live with ambiguity, willing to say "I don't know" about almost everything—the effects of intercessory prayer, the legitimacy of war, the normalcy of homosexuality, the nature of biblical writings, or even the nature of God. To think this way makes for a broad tolerance of differences, and for honesty, but it is also unsettling. I see it as a part of what it means to "live by faith, not by sight."

It is true that by nature it is easier for some people to live with ambiguity than it is for others. Some are more comfortable with "black or white" in their mode of thinking. Unfortunately, it is also true that it is not easy for these two types of people to appreciate each other!

The Creator is also the Lover

From nature and by nature we can know the power and
orderliness of God, but what is new and startling about
the Judaeo-Christian understanding of God is that God is
a moral God (hating evil, loving good behavior) and a God
of love, compassion and forgiveness. This is the excitement
and novelty of the Gospel. And this is evidenced by
the Christian's experience. There is not only power and
wisdom in the universe—but there is Someone who loves
me!

   O great God, I am overwhelmed with your explosive
creative power and your tender intimacy which envelop me
at the same time!

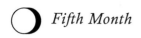

The Way of resurrection

It's all about resurrection! What Jesus, the Christ sent from God, represents is indestructible! Try to kill it and it comes right back to life, because it is of God.

What did Jesus represent? Love, healing, willingness to sacrifice all for truth and justice, stewardship of life as a gift, openness to God's Spirit over against a closed system of clericalism and ritualism and arrogance and oppressive rule.

The "new covenant in my blood" proclaims: "Away with the old system of God as Lawgiver and Judge! I'm showing you a new Way. Just follow me! I am willing to sacrifice my life in order to be completely open and obedient to the Heavenly Voice. It will all come out right in the end!

"Now, come everyone and participate in my Way! It is the Way of resurrection. It absolutely will come out all right in the end. Share my life! I am the vine, you are the branches; the Father is in me and I in you. If you are open and obedient, no matter what troubles might assail you, in the end resurrection awaits you!"

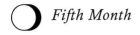

We cannot confine the Word of God

Unorthodox as it may sound to many, perhaps we would do well not to call the Bible "the Word of God," because the historical and literary factors in the composition of this book are such that some strata contain some idiosyncrasies and warped religious views of ancient cultures, views which we cannot reconcile with the voice of God as we know it in Christ. Think of the heartlessly cruel injunctions that came as the word of the Lord to Israel as she was trying to capture the Promised Land in the days of the Judges.

The word that God is still speaking today is not something confined to the concepts that prevailed more than a millenium before Christ. There is a wonderful freedom about the word that God speaks; it surprises us by its newness, freshness, creativeness. What a blessing it is to listen for what God has to say to us today! It is rooted in biblical themes, but not confined to the words of the ancient biblical writers, many of which were quite contrary to the spirit of Jesus, the Word made flesh.

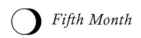 *Fifth Month*

Second Week   Thursday   *Lord's Prayer*

Grand concepts of the Lord's Prayer

We pray, "Thy Kingdom come, Thy will be done on earth...." These two words—kingdom and earth—are big, grandiose, all encompassing words. This prayer is not about something small, private or exclusive, but breathes an expansive, social, national, global nuance—a kingdom for planet earth.

In praying this prayer, we do not image God's work among us as a kind of private salvation for people who think a certain way. No, we see God's work as a kingdom, a realm vast in scope and power.

We do not pray, "Thy will be done in my heart," nor in our church. No, we pray that God's will might be done in the whole earth. The health of planet earth is included in this prayer: "May all nature and history be functioning according to your will."

Second Week   Friday   *Human Condition*

Waiting—too long

Procrastination is a symptom of perfectionism, which is a symptom of neuroticism. For procrastination says: Don't do it unless you can do it perfectly, and since you can't do it perfectly now, you'd better wait—and wait, and wait!

This frame of mind is also disastrous for faith, for it also operates in prayer. It says: Don't pray now because you don't feel like saying a proper prayer. Don't open to faith now, because you're not fit for it at the moment, so wait—and wait, and wait! Finally the opportunity for change is lost altogether.

Lord, deliver us from that deadly sin—procrastination!

Third Week   Monday   *Nature of God*

The One beyond space and time

The most inherent character of the universe as we know it and human life within that universe is that we are bound within time and within space. We cannot think of our existence outside these two "givens." But sages and religions talk about an eternal God, and a God who lives "in heaven" or "above the heavens." I.e., they see God as one who is NOT bound by time or space. Indeed, if God is truly different than human beings, then this is what distinguishes God. He is of a completely different order of things, an order where one can be everywhere at once, and where one has no beginning or end.

No one has seen God or the divine form or the divine mind, yet theologians and preachers too often try to define God and the way God works in human life and in the world by our doctrines of creation, redemption, salvation, Trinity, etc. But if God's nature is a mystery, it follows that our theological dogma should be more tentative, more humble, more awe-filled.

Let us quiet our dogmatics and be silent before the holy God.

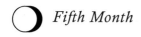

Third Week   *Tuesday*   *Resurrection*

"Why hast thou forsaken me?"

When Jesus cried out from the cross, "My God, my God, why hast thou forsaken me?" God had indeed forsaken Jesus, because in Jesus' death, the personification of Good was being destroyed by the opponents of this Good One. The Good had been forsaken by God. Whenever I oppose the Good, I am on the side of those who were destroying the Good One. I am indeed nailing him to the cross.

But who was raised on the third day? Simply the Good come back again? On one level we might say that Jesus was raised by God not only as a sign that Good cannot be destroyed, but that the Good will unexpectedly spring back again.

However, the drama of crucifixion and resurrection has a dimension even deeper than this. Jesus died in faith in and obedience to God. He did good not just for the sake of doing good, but for the sake of obedience to God (who does indeed will only good.)

So Jesus was raised by God as the outcome of his perfect obedience to the call of God. Faith and commitment can never be destroyed!

Our Jewish heritage

"Save us, O Lord our God, and gather us from the nations, that we may give thanks to your holy name and glory in your praise." (Psalm 106:47) These words seem to sum up the message of the Psalms and express the "world view" of the ancient Israelites. They were conscious of their uniqueness, their "chosen-ness" ("gathered us from the nations") because they worshipped the invisible, living God, while all the other nations worshipped man-made idols and lived by ethical standards far inferior to the high standards of the Ten Commandments.

God was in a centuries-long process of shaping Israel to be God's people, a people that would bring praise and glory to the true God.

This is the heritage we have as the Christian church, as a people living in the stream of the unique revelation of God's self as creator of heaven and earth. That revelation began with Abraham and culminated in Jesus, the Christ, and continues today.

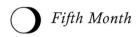

Third Week   Thursday   *Lord's Prayer*

"Thy will" and my action

I tend to get hung up in abstractions when I pray,
"Our Father who art in heaven, Hallowed be thy name."
The place called "heaven," and the idea of "Hallowing the
name" seem so abstract. How do those big concepts relate
to my daily activities of the present time?

Then I go on: "Thy will be done…" Ah, this is different;
this talks about doing, deciding.

Willing, deciding, doing mean activity. So here "thy will"
links into concrete, everyday action. This is a petition about
everyday life, as I aim to do what is right from moment to
moment, hour to hour. The prayer suddenly becomes very
practical. I pray that all my actions may be in accordance
with what is right in the divine perspective.

And when I live that way, and the whole community also
tries to live that way, that is the "Kingdom of God" coming.

Third Week   Friday   *Reflections*

On growing old

When I was thinking rather cynically about the
meaninglessness of continuing to live as we grow old,
this thought struck me: I'm placed in this extraordinarily
beautiful, intricately created earth to enjoy it and be
grateful for it. Maybe my Creator wants me to live as long
as possible just to rejoice and be thankful to him for the
wonderful world God has made. Not to do this would be
an insult to God.

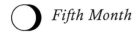

God communicates

I have stumbled at the idea of God as a God who reveals himself, who communicates with human beings. However, God is necessarily capable of doing all and more than God's created human beings can do—and we can communicate! If we can communicate ourselves to others, as we constantly do to a greater or lesser extent, then it is surely not surprising that the Creator can do as much as the creatures.

Speak, Lord, for we are listening!

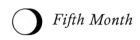

Jesus, the revolutionary

The life and death of Jesus is the pivotal point which gave birth to a new perception of the work of God as being an all-inclusive work, a blessing for all people. Up to that point, the conception of God's work had been an exclusive one, i.e., it was understood as a revelation of God to the chosen people Israel, to the Jews. The Jewish religion was bounded by the Law of Moses, embedded in the Temple and the Torah.

The turning point was in the crucifixion of Jesus where Jesus enacted a new kind of bond/covenant between God and the human family, one based on perfect obedience of Jesus to the Father's will. That obedience led to his death, and that death supplanted the countless deaths of animals sacrificed in the Jewish religious system. It supplanted the Temple and the Torah as the way of salvation.

Paul's understanding and his mission did much to solidify the new understanding of the God-human relationship (the covenant) as one that soared beyond Jewish doctrinal boundaries, beyond Jewish ethnic boundaries. We now understand that the New Covenant is universal in scope and open to all, for it is focused on "the Jesus Way."

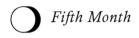

A symphony of voices

A fundamentalist single-dimension view of the Bible as simply—from beginning to end—"the word of God" leaves the Bible flat and uninteresting. That view sees the whole Bible as being on the same "pitch" (as in music), and this sadly undermines the rich variety of views, the symphony of voices expressed by the many writers and contexts in which the books were written.

The Bible is highly multi-dimensional, so we can see the revelation of God from many angles. It is like the blind men examining an elephant and each finding different phenomena—the leg, the tail, the trunk, etc.—and foolishly concluding that their own perception was the whole. The reality of the whole elephant was something much more wonderful than either of them understood on their own.

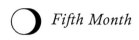

A different kind of universe?

Heaven is a key word common to both of the first two petitions—"Father in heaven, hallowed be thy name" and "Thy will be done on earth as in heaven." This word, that refers to what we must call an "unknown," must, nevertheless, bear considerable significance.

If God is great and mysterious enough to create this awesome universe—and the creative process is absolutely incomprehensible, and evolutionary theory does nothing to lessen the mystery—then that God is also great and mysterious enough to create a completely different kind of universe as well—one which is a place of perfect spirit and beauty and glorious life, without flaws, without limitations. It is, indeed, the very place—if it is a place at all—where God dwells.

That's the place we call "heaven," and Jesus teaches that it can be integrated into our everyday life: "Thy will be done on earth as in heaven."

The penultimate is not the ultimate

Religion vs. ultimate truth might be illustrated by two concentric circles with human beings in the center. The inner circle is religion, with its accompaniment of dogma and ritual. The outer circle is sacred reality itself, the ultimate truth. The activities of the inner circle point to and in some measure reflect the outer circle.

Unfortunately, it is all too easy for us to think that the inner circle is an end in itself, but it is only the penultimate, (next to the last) not the ultimate. It is idolatry to let the penultimate deceive us into treating is as the ultimate.

Sixth Month

Extraterrestrial encounter

Oil, 2009

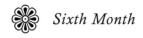

First Week   Monday   Nature of God

God as the totality

Should we conceive of God as the sum total of all the time and space and things of the universe? Maybe that comes close—closer anyway than the concept of a divine Being sitting in some remote corner of that universe.

But things or beings are the only kinds of existence our human minds can grasp. So if God is not a being, much less a thing, then what can God be?

We sense that God must be primarily spirit. That puts God in the realm of intangibles, intangible just as human consciousness is intangible. So is God then perhaps the primal consciousness, or the sum total of all consciousness in the universe? Is that a legitimate way to conceive of the Holy Spirit?

Yet this spiritual God is immanent in the world, not separated from the created world. Science continually reveals the complexity and awesomeness of the created world. So let us take this as a dim reflection of the complexity and awesomeness of God.

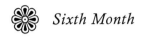

First Week   *Tuesday*   *The Cross event*

The radical newness of Jesus

The New Testament and Jesus must be understood in
the context of the Old Testament. In that light we see the
revolutionary character of Jesus. For example, central to
the OT way of life was the sacrificial system, whereby the
sinner took the initiative to bring a lamb or bird, lay his
hand on its head, offer it up by killing it—killing one of
his own valuable animals. But that act and the aroma of
that offering were promised to appease God's anger at the
sinner so sin could be forgiven.

Now see Jesus as a Jew in that stream of religiosity—
Jesus, who sees himself as the promised Messiah from God.
This Jesus let himself be killed and in that very moment
says, "Father forgive them, for they do not know what
they are doing." Jesus took the initiative; Jesus offered
forgiveness even to those who were not repentant. That is
amazing grace, unmerited acceptance, unconditional love!

In the OT system, the penitent took an unwilling animal
and offered it up, killing it on the altar. The life was in the
blood. But Jesus *willingly* offered his own self for penitents.

Substitutionary atonement theory is a tit for tat concept
of God—Jesus takes the punishment and I get forgiveness.
But Jesus' way was not tit for tat, neither vindictive, neither
violent, but the epitome of unconditional love for all. Jesus
proved the sacrifices to be unnecessary by his taking the
initiative of unconditional love.

Let us be sure we are living in the age of the New
Covenant, and not still under the Old!

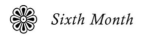

A contemporary meaning of "New Covenant"

Reading Joshua and the Old Testament stories, it is clear that the "old covenant" was one of violent revenge and killing of enemies. On that last night of Jesus' life, he said, "This is the new covenant in my blood…" Should we not take that to mean, "I am about to demonstrate a revolutionary way of coping with the evils of life, the way of self-sacrifice rather than the way of revenge. The old way didn't work; I shall provide an entirely new way."

If we apply the truth implied in this new covenant to our present day, it means that respect for other nations, even "enemy nations," with consequent efforts at diplomatic negotiation, rather than violent vengeance and deadly militarism should characterize the Christian approach to current international relations.

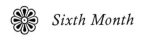

First Week   *Thursday*   *Lord's Prayer*

Ask!

I usually do not ask for specific things in prayer, but just give thanks and praise and pray for spiritual openness, etc. However, "Give us our daily bread" is here in the model prayer, and this encourages us to ask for gifts—"Please give us…" When we do that, it forces us to focus on what we really want. This is a good exercise in setting priorities.

It also gives goals and challenge to my relation to God: Does God really hear my heart's desire? Does God actually give me the "daily bread" I ask for? Such an expectant attitude puts concreteness, particularity and excitement into what can otherwise become a vague "spirituality."

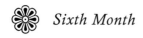

Parable of two farmers

The Christian's life is not a "state of salvation," a static condition of being a different kind of humanity. Both the Christian and non-Christian are the same human beings, subject to temptations and despair, often failing in their purpose. But what is different about Christians' experience is that they are daily forgiven for the darkness of soul, and get a new lease on life.

Think of the analogy of two Nebraska farm homes side by side. Both farmers are subject to the same heat and dust and grime, and get equally dirty every day. But in one home the farmer takes a daily shower and washes off the day's soil, puts on clean overalls and begins fresh every morning with hope for a better day.

The other farmer never takes a bath or changes his clothes and gets dirtier and more grimy, with less self-respect and greater discouragement with every day that passes. The two households are not different states of being. They live in the same world with the same dirt. Yet the two households will doubtlessly have very different attitudes and feelings, because of doing or not doing the daily washing.

Daily cleansing of our spirit can make a world of difference.

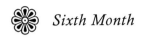

Second Week   Monday   *Nature of God*

Why "Heavenly Father"

"Heavenly Father" is the traditional Christian term for God. The immediate impact of these words on our imagination is a kindly male person residing in some distant celestial place controlling the world. But this figure, although it may satisfy a pious conservative person, no longer satisfies most of us. The holocaust and the many natural disaster which are such cruel events, make belief in such a God impossible.

Yet it was none other than Jesus who taught us to pray, "Our Father in heaven." So how do we understand these words? Perhaps these are the only words available to describe the reality of God without writing a philosophical treatise on the subject.

What is that reality? "Father" is an originator/progenitor, creator/creative power of human life, a force that is personal, conscious, working toward the good. And heaven is another sphere from the earth surrounding us, not necessarily a place, but a spiritual arena.

Put these two together and we get some concept of the kind of God we believe in. "Heavenly Father" is the succinct abbreviation for all this.

The reason why it is urgent to make this kind of interpretation is that the "Grandfather in the sky" image doesn't work, and so people in great numbers become atheistic or agnostic. They ridicule Christians for their nonsensical irrational belief in a good heavenly Being who is controlling the universe.

Many today are sensitive to the gender issue in referring to God. Why have we always used the term "Father" rather than "Mother"? The same characteristics as mentioned above can apply equally to a mother. Perhaps in the not too

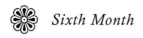

distant future the church will be using "gender-neutral" terms for God.

If we want thinking people to remain in the community of faith we must offer them some way of thinking about God that makes more sense than the old paradigm.

Second Week   Tuesday   The Cross event

Christus Victor

Seeing that Jesus died because of our sins rather than for our sins, as many theologians are saying these days, is in line with that alternative view of what happened on the cross proffered by the Swedish theologian Gustav Aulen in his Christus Victor theory of the atonement. In this approach, the essence of redemption is found not in a sacrificial offering but in a battle with the power of sin.

Second Week   Wednesday   Scripture

Job speaks to us

The overall point of the book of Job in the OT is that true religion is different from morality. Religion is on a deeper level than simply ethical living. Job's three friends saw his suffering only in terms of morality, i.e., that his suffering is the result of his sin. But Job insists they are wrong. The conclusion of the book is that there is a deeper dimension to life—the realm of mystery, that goes beyond a moralistic tit for tat view of sin and punishment. As Job shows in his final speech, his suffering points to a dimension that, in fact, no human being can comprehend.

That is true religion. Would that we all could see our suffering in this light.

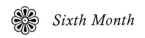

Second Week　　*Thursday*　　　　　　　*Lord's Prayer*

All is "gift"

The form of this petition—"Give us"—reminds us that all our daily necessities, beginning with the food we need to sustain life, are things given to us, that is, gifts. As such, they should never be taken for granted. Are they really gifts? Aren't they our own possessions? They are "gift" because we did not create or originate any of the life processes. The growth of plants from seeds, the birth and growth of animals by the mysterious process of conception—it all originates in the Higher Power, in God, who has gifted the human race with all the resources and marvels that sustain our life.

These words contain also a second matter of great significance: they are in the plural—"us", "our." We pray that all people will be given these gifts. The back side of this petition is, therefore, that we are challenged to share what we have received so that the gifts of material goods, beginning with food, can be enjoyed by all the human family.

There is a powerful moral imperative here for us to work to eliminate hunger in our own country and in the world, and to make political provision for the just distribution of these material goods.

Tell it like it is!

"Original sin," a standard phrase in theological vocabulary, but one much maligned by modern Christians, is nothing other than the everyday reality that I don't love God, I don't desire God's presence in my life with all my heart. Closely related to this is the fact that I don't want to think deeply about ultimate goals and values—it's too troublesome, too uncomfortable.

There is nothing I can do about this other than tell it like it is, i.e., confess this reality and ask for divine intervention in spite of all my negative feeling, because I do want to honor the Eternal One, the Maker of heaven and earth, and want to live for long-range goals.

When I do that, a silent change occurs, and a more receptive and humble self begins to peep out.

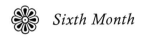

Third Week   *Monday*   *God*

God is a self-revealing God

A fundamental Christian belief about God is that God is a self-revealing God. This is, after all, the meaning of God's "calling" of Abraham and the patriarchs, of God's "speaking" to Moses giving him the Law, of the Torah as expressing God's will, of God's speaking through the prophets, and finally of Jesus' coming as the "Word made flesh." Because of this belief about God being a "self-revealing" God, we can call the Bible—the account of these various revelations—the "Word of God." And we also believe the Holy Spirit is the continuing power of God's communication to the human race. Yes, "God is still speaking."

Third Week   *Tuesday*   *The Cross event*

Ascension theory

The writer of the Fourth Gospel does not uphold or in any way proclaim the sacrificial atonement theory as later espoused by Paul. John is full of positive images; Christ is Light and Life from beginning to end. He is vividly aware of evil in the world, but is satisfied to say that God in Christ overcomes evil.

Perhaps we can say that John takes the "Ascension Theory" rather than "Atonement Theory." The ascended Lord is doing mighty wonders for us.

God's anger and pleasure

The view of God as a God angry with his people is a prominent theme of the Old Testament. Most Christians have chosen to overlook the idea of an angry God.

Did God's character change after the time of Jesus? Or was there a general misunderstanding of God's nature among the ancients which Jesus rectified?

The general view of the Old Testament is that of a God whose anger causes human trouble and suffering and whose constant love and saving help cause human deliverance and happiness.

Viewed negatively, this seems like a very simplistic, anthropomorphic view of God. Is God simply like human beings who occasionally vent their anger, and then are sorry and show some compassion?

But viewed positively, the biblical writers understand both individual and national history to be ruled by God. Both in the valleys of suffering as well as in the peaks of blessing, every event, good and bad, was in the hand of God. Suffering they saw as "divine anger;" blessing they saw as divine good will.

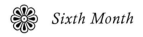

Third Week   *Thursday*   *Lord's Prayer*

The Kingdom: bread and forgiveness

We pray in the Lord's Prayer, "Thy Kingdom come," and interpret that with the next phrase, "Thy will be done." Where the will of God is done, there is the Kingdom. The following petitions of the Lord's Prayer define what the Kingdom and the will of God actually are. "Give us this day our daily bread" suggests the priority of trustingly and thankfully looking to God to supply human need day by day, rather than laying up treasures and worrying about material things. What kind of economic theory should be built on this?

And secondly, the Kingdom is about forgiveness—being forgiven and forgiving others. This is profound. When we pray, "Forgive us" it implies that we trust God is a forgiving God and will give us a new chance to start over every day. Forgiveness is what gives hope; these are two sides of a coin. They stand in opposition to despair. "As we forgive others..." is also an ethical imperative and a directive for maintaining healthy relationships. This is as important as bread for our bodies.

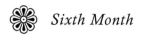

Third Week   Friday   The Way

Three ways to experience the will of God

When we pray "Thy will be done," and earnestly desire to
see the will of God carried out in the world, it is important
to remember that God's will is carried out in at least three
distinct dimensions: the individual, the social and the
natural. I.e., God's will is done in my individual life, and
it is done in the way people relate to each other in the
structures of society, and it is also done in the world of
nature, in the whole universe.

I have individual responsibility to strive to do the will
of God in my own life. But also, I, as a member of society,
have responsibility to influence the structure of society so
that it can be a better instrument of God's will for a just
social order. And perhaps the wonderful world of nature is
the most submissive to the will of God, its creator.

May God give me grace to be as submissive and as
faithful to the divine way as the mighty oak tree in our
neighborhood!

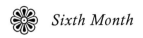

Fourth Week   Monday   *God*

Who is at the center?

It seems there are two distinct understandings of the relation of God and human beings: One, often the position taken by the academics, sees human beings at the center, and the realm of God and spiritual things can be seen as human projections. Philosophers create concepts of the world of Spirit. Theologians create the ideas of heaven and life after death, ideas of a "kingdom of God." These things we have created through our human potential constitute religion and the religious way of life.

The other understanding of the relation of God and humanity, usually the position taken by biblically oriented persons, sees God at the center and at the beginning. God is the mysterious unknowable One behind the galaxies, behind quarks and behind the Big Bang. God creates mankind. Humanity and the world we know are just one little piece of the grand whole. Our reasoning and intellect are wonderful instruments, but they are utterly finite, unable to grasp the grand whole.

May God give us the humility to realize we are not the central figures in the universe!

Fourth Week   *Tuesday*   *The Cross event*

Was Jesus confused?

"If you don't have a sword, sell your cloak and buy one," said Jesus during the time of his final suffering (Luke 22). Such strange words from his lips! How shall we reconcile these words to the rest of Jesus' sayings? Looking at Jesus in his complete humanity, is it wrong to think that he must have been utterly confused about what was happening?

He might have foreseen it clearly hours and days before, but now that deniers, betrayers, armed soldiers and jeering crowds were assailing him, everything got cloudy, upset and confusion temporarily reigned.

Likewise, can we not see the same confusion in the words from the cross: "My God, my God, why have you forsaken me!" and a little later, "Father, into your hands I commit my spirit." These two expressions could hardly be more contrary in the feelings expressed.

To recognize these tormented feelings in Jesus is to recognize his true humanity. We see on the cross a human being like ourselves, suffering in body, mind and spirit! Yes, he was a martyr—and more than a martyr!

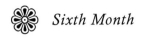

The "wrath of God" in the Psalms

It is easy to be offended by the frequent portrayal of God as being wrathful and vindictive in dealing with the human family. But there is something reassuring about this view. The distinctive thing about the attitude of the psalmist is that he sees all his inner pain, desperation and suffering as being related to or stemming from God. He feels God is angry with him. However, from this same God he also expects ultimate rescue from all his troubles. But for the time being the only salvation is to wait. So waiting becomes a frequent motif in the Psalms.

The important thing is that the writer never lets his misery separate him from God. He never completely despairs, for God is there. What a contrast this view is from our age of secularism and science, where we strive for a non-religious world view, a world without God.

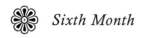

Fourth Week   *Thursday*   *The Way*

Our sin—personal and social

When we pray the Lord's Prayer and come to "Forgive us..." the tone of the prayer becomes very personal. In dealing with trespasses, i.e., with wrongdoing and sin, we are dealing with our personal life experiences. When I ask for forgiveness, I'm expected to uncover my moral life, the actions that make me feel guilty.

But there is more. Much of our wrongdoing is not the result of my personal wayward decision, but is the result of living in a society and a political order that has made wrong choices. The injustice, the military violence, the self-seeking nature of our powerful government vis a vis other nations of the world—we are willy-nilly supporting, through taxes and other means, this society that is fraught with so much that is contrary to the will of God. We need to ask God's forgiveness also for this aspect of our sinfulness.

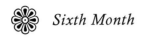

Fourth Week   Friday   *Commitment*

Air and water as metaphor

Grace is like air; it's always pushing in on me, but I
must take a breath in order for it to maintain my life. In
swimming, water is a metaphor of darkness. I must turn
my face up to breathe doing the crawl, or lie on my back
in order to receive the life-giving air. If I don't, I'm quickly
dead. Just so there seems to be another everywhere-present
but unseen force waiting to drown me unless I deliberately
breathe in the air of the spirit.

Grace is not a power that overwhelms us. Jesus is the
bread of life that must be eaten, the life-giving oxygen that
must be inhaled.

If we want to be close to God, we must live proactively.

Seventh Month

Iyashi (Japanese ideograph meaning "healing")

Oil, 2009

"Not the God of Philosophers"

Pascal used this phrase in describing the Christian God: "Not the God of the philosophers, but the God of Abraham, Isaac and Jacob." That God calls us, speaks to us; that God is the One of whom St. John wrote, "God is love."

The Judaeo-Christian tradition points to the way of love, not the way of philosophical analysis. We are called not to analyze but to love. Love is the core of the Mystery.

This is the implication of Pascal's insistence that we should revere not a philosophical construct, but reverence the Leader, Guide and Friend of historical persons—Abraham, Isaac and Jacob.

Have we lost the newness of the Gospel?

Forgiveness points to a miracle in relationships, a supra-natural act. It means the natural cycle of wrong-doing/revenge is broken rather than escalated. The concept of the Jewish sacrificial system was that the only way to break the cycle was by paying for redemption, as by offering a sacrifice.

The logic went like this: Sin brings punishment; this is a kind of law of the moral realm. God demands some kind of pay in order to redeem the sinner. But Jesus stepped in and took the punishment on himself, i.e., he paid the price of sacrifice himself, so now we can be freed from the punishment. What we see in Jesus was a new form of the Old Testament ritual.

But let's take another look at that. Is it right that we should see the forgiving love of God in these terms of fulfilling the cycle of sin/punishment/sacrifice? Or should we recognize in the work of Christ a truly New Covenant, a "new arrangement," in which God does an astonishing new thing through the coming of Jesus, his Promised One?

What is that new thing? It is that the old sin/punishment/paying for redemption cycle is *broken*. The whole old system was done away with by a new one, a new understanding of God. God's nature is not a vicious, demanding one; Jesus showed God to be full of mercy, grace and forgiveness.

If we say that Jesus' death was a sacrifice for sin that satisfied God's justice so that God can now forgive, we are still seeing God through the lens of the Old Covenant. Let's not lose the wonderful newness of the Gospel!

Romans 8 and Process Theology

The powerful theme of the 8th chapter of Romans is that "Nothing can separate us from the love of God." Isn't this actually saying the same thing as Process Theology says about God, namely, that the beneficent God is always and everywhere present in the whole universe ? That is the essence of the "panentheism" of Process Theology. We can be absolutely safe and secure in the all-embracing arms of the One who gave us life.

Forgive us as we forgive

We pray in the Lord's Prayer: "Forgive us our sins as we forgive those who sin against us." We live by forgiveness. We are never perfect, yet that does not disqualify us from God's constant grace. Our lives, for either biological or social or environmental reasons, might be lived in a "second best" manner from beginning to end, but even that does not exclude us from God's forgiving love.

And the twist in this petition is that this same kind of long-suffering, tolerant attitude must also characterize our relations with one another, which likewise are never perfect. Here is a word of great comfort integrated with a great challenge! Let us live this day in the spirit of forgiveness.

Just to keep alive?

Occasionally when I fill my pill box each week, it makes me wistfully philosophical, and I ask, Why am I doing this? Am I taking these expensive pills just to keep alive? Just to keep alive is not a very good reason to continue spending money for medications. Wasn't it better in the days before modern medicine, when people just naturally died when they reached their 70s and 80s? Why use up the earth's resources when we're no longer being productive, and when young people need those resources more than we do?

Care for health is surely a fundamental responsibility, but in our later years there comes a time and a bodily condition when it might be good to stop and examine the meaning of life. Maintaining my physical body, important as that is, must be balanced with other factors involving family and community, use of money and other resources.

Are we ready for divine intervention?

I believe there are times when God acts through interventions in the processes of the natural world, much as our scientific age would like to deny even the possibility of such intervention. We cannot predict these interventions, but they are what proves faith to be real.

God is hidden; God's will and ways are hidden, God's "location" in the universe is hidden. But occasionally the divine peeks out from behind the veil of hiddenness and surprises us.

And we must admit that even this is subject to interpretation. I might look at a certain event—healing, for example—and say, "This is an act of God," while my friend might look at the same event and say, "Pure coincidence."

The event of Jesus—his life and death and resurrection—offers the archetype of divine intervention in history. This event is a wonderful story of the way God works in the world. I.e., God appears in unexpected places at unexpected times, in an unexpected manner.

Am I ready for a visit from God today!

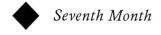

Jesus the Savior

I am returning to an appreciation of the title "Savior" for Jesus. In my youth, "Savior" was a wonderful word filled with emotion and tears of gratitude—"I have found Jesus as my Savior" marked the decisive experience of a true believer. However, later the constant use of this word in religious vocabulary became trite, meaningless and even offensive. I never used it.

But recently it has come back to me as a profound expression of what the whole Incarnation reality is all about. The whole Christ event takes us from darkness and despair to light and overwhelming joy. It saves us from ugliness and despair.

In that context Jesus is the *Christus Victor*, the Savior who underwent all the hardships of persecutions during his lifetime, and then suffered death and rose from the dead—not because he deserved it, but for us. Yes, he is a wonderful friend and helper, but more than just a helper— an eternal savior who completely transforms us. I feel him personally at my side defending me, comforting me, encouraging and leading me.

Second Week   Wednesday   *Scripture*

Religion at the center

The assumption of the Old Testament, take Isaiah 46 as an example, is a context of a theocratic society. Religion was at the center of everything. So the big issue for the Israelites was whether to worship Yahweh or to worship some other gods.

But we live in a secular society. Religion and gods—much less God—are not central; individuals and their material culture are central. As it stands, can the Old Testament be relevant to our secular society? How do we bridge the gap so the language and concepts of the Bible can be meaningful to us?

I sometimes think we need a whole new story of the divine-human encounter, a whole new Bible, if you will, one that would not be so hard to "translate" into a contemporary mode of communication!

Second Week   Thursday   *Prayer*

My last prayer

At my last hour of life I want to be able to say, "Father, into your hands I commit my spirit." If that prayer was appropriate for Jesus at the moment of his death on the cross, it is also appropriate for me.

And next I want to pray, "Lord of my life and my death, astonish me now!" For what will happen after the moment of death remains a deep mystery. I eagerly anticipate an astonishing surprise !

Newton's apple—and us

When Isaac Newton saw the apple fall from the tree that one, critical time, he saw an old, common occurrence in a new light that revolutionized the world. Newton's theory of gravity that stemmed from that experience, ushered us into a new age of science.

Sometimes, by the working of the divine Spirit, we see old, common occurrences in a completely new light, and our lives can be revolutionized. Who knows what you might see in the falling of an apple today!

Evolution of the concept of God

The Old Testament can be seen as a book of primitive religion, an expression of the early evolution of monotheism. Old Testament religion sees God as a great king who controls all that happens, gives good things to those who worship him and do good, and metes out punishment in the form of suffering to those who worship other gods and do evil things. That God has a favored people, the Jews, and constantly shows them special favor. Some interpret this as a kind of primitive tribal religion.

In contrast, Christianity can be seen as a much more profound religion, with a universal outlook and spiritual base. Its central theme is unconditional love, of God for humanity and of human beings for one another. How hard it has been through the centuries to follow this higher path! How easy to slip back into the primitive mode of believing in a "tit for tat" God sitting on his throne up there someplace, holding a moral scale that plays favoritism and punishes people when they're bad and rewards them when they're good.

Let us pray that God will reveal God's true nature to us day by day.

Third Week   *Tuesday*   *The Cross event*

He saved others, but not himself

The whole of the Gospel story, in all its paradoxes, is epitomized in the scoffing of those assailing Jesus on the cross: "He saved others, he cannot save himself. If he is God's Son, let him come down from the cross and we will believe."

The secret of salvation in Christ is hidden in the fact that he did not come down, did not save himself. Why? Could he have done so? As a man this would hardly have been possible. But if he was indeed God in the flesh, he would have been able to save himself. But as the manifestation of God he chose not to do so, but rather to go all the way with humanity. Thus Jesus, the revelation of God, could not save himself at that crucial moment of history. But this is precisely how he showed the sacrificial love of God for humanity.

Amazing grace!

Vessels for understanding

Paul's concepts of justification, reconciliation, first and second Adam, etc. (Romans 5) are a kind of "vehicle" by which we can find some understanding of the God-man relationships. They are like boxes or vessels with a specific shape in which we give structure to an idea. These ideas give "shape" to faith and feelings. Without some such vehicle with a definite shape, our faith would be like formless and ephemeral fog on a misty morning.

To think that we can make some particular box that is the absolutely perfect shape would be idolatry. We must be constantly building new boxes as our world changes and as people's world view changes.

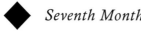

Third Week   Thursday   Human condition

Stop and think!

When we fail to stop and think and reflect about what we are doing we get into a rut, and sheer momentum keeps us going on the track we started. But we could be going the wrong direction, and a change in course might be needed. It is only natural to allow ourselves to be controlled by momentum. Sometimes this is a positive thrust, but it can also hinder us from being creative and innovative. Thinking is hard; it takes effort; it makes us swim upstream.

It takes a disciplined effort to quiet ourselves, to stop and take time to listen to our heart and conscience, to hear the voice of the Spirit. Practices such as deep breathing or Tai-chi can be of great help. They slow us down and relax the body and mind; this quells the static and prepares our ears to hear.

Third Week   Friday   Reflections

Disney Hall as metaphor

How wonderful the experience of a concert in Disney Hall at the Los Angeles Music Center! Fabulous, inspiring music pouring forth from one of the world's great orchestras fills the hall for two hours. At the end there is the excitement of several thousand people exuberantly giving the performers a standing ovation.

But within ten minutes the hall is empty, quiet, deserted; the experience of that music is gone forever, never to be repeated just that way again.

Is not this a melancholy symbol of our life—ecstatic today, silent tomorrow, vibrant today, nothing left tomorrow?

God is in my neighbor

If God is immanent in me and in all creation, then God is a presence in all human beings. So loving God necessarily commits me to loving my neighbor. In fact, the only way I can love God is by loving my neighbor.

It is often said that we see Christ in our neighbor. Indeed, if the risen Christ is everywhere present in the world today, then, literally, we see Christ in our neighbor.

The same logic applies to the idea of being open to God and being open to others. If God is everywhere present, God is in my neighbor, so when I am open to my neighbor, I am open to God.

O God open my eyes to see you today!

Fourth Week   Tuesday   *Jesus Christ*

First look at context

The saying of Jesus, "I am the Way....No one comes to the Father but by me" is a stumbling block for many—both for those who have never known the Jesus Way, and for those engaged in inter-faith dialogue. It is important to remember that this was not a statement made in the context of a discussion with individuals who were born into other religious traditions.

So neither should it be used by Christians as though it were a hard steel shield as we face people of good will in other religions—fighting off all other religious claims. It is quite possible that Jesus did not even know about other religions. But he did know Judaism, and he was addressing Jewish people when he said these words.

He was saying to the Jews: "I am the fulfillment of the Old Covenant; in me is a new covenant between God and human beings. Come follow me in the New Way!"

Likewise *for us* Jesus is the Way to God. And his Way is our Way; thus the sub-title of this book.

Fourth Week   Wednesday   *The Way*

The revolutionary Good Samaritan

This most well known parable of Jesus teaches a wonderful, but revolutionary, ethic. The questioner's mind-set, "Who is my neighbor?" indicates a concern for the proper stratification of society. The question was, "To what kind of people ought I to be kind and helpful?"

But the parable of the foreigner who did good to a total stranger, with its revolutionary twist at the end—"Go and do likewise"—proclaims a new ethic: "You take the initiative to upset the social strata; don't wait for others to be decent to you. You start the cycle of good will! If you don't start, everyone will sit back waiting for others to start being neighborly, and nothing positive will ever occur.

We can find such a revolutionary twist at the end of many of Jesus' parables.

The way of the Good Samaritan is not an easy path. God, help me to follow his path today!

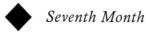

Self esteem vs. selfishness

For many conscientious Christians, self esteem and selfishness are often distorted in the process of our development. I see it in myself. We fear being ourselves, because this seems to be selfishness, which creates guilt on the basis of Christian morality. The difficulty is in drawing the line between what is really selfishness and what is proper concern for my best welfare.

In Freudian terms, the problem could be stated in terms of selfishness as the function of the id, self-effacement as the work of the super-ego, with proper self esteem as the function of the ego. It is not easy to walk the razor-edge of rational ego control, avoiding both extremes of id and super-ego. A self-effacing kindness might simply pamper another person's selfishness and dependency. But a focus on self-esteem can be conceit and vanity. Neither extreme fulfills the goal of healthy personhood. Where do you stand on the scale of psychological health?

The arts are windows

The arts—music, painting, literature, architecture, dance, and all the rest—can be metaphors of things divine in our midst. If we have the will to see it, they are pointers to God. They can be windows to give us a glimpse of the Holy Spirit. The arts, although they have a material form, are in essence spiritual, and they appeal to our spiritual nature.

Esthetic sense is a kind of intuition, a sense of something beyond intellectual description. And is it not also intuition that leads us to sense God in our life? The nurture of the artistic in life is important for fostering our spirituality.

When was the last time you intentionally opened your eyes and ears to the spiritual quality of the beauty surrounding you?

Eighth Month

An Afghan youth in Claremont

Oil, 2010

Creeds and computer icons

There are many words and sentences of the creeds, of
Christian dogma, or of the Bible that are like the icons
on my computer screen. Those icons are little codes or
keys that allow us to enter programs and functions of
the computer. Likewise, the phrases we use in religious
language are not meant to be "the truth," or the whole
content of faith. Rather, we should take them as the icons or
buttons on the computer screen. When we press a button it
opens up a wealth of detailed information.

So in our theological thinking we need to ask, What is
the rich, many-sided, meaning of such phrases as "Triune
God," "the Kingdom of God," or "atonement," or "seated
at the right hand of God" and so forth? We should take
these phrases to be windows that open up into a larger
understanding of God's ways.

May we have the patience and diligence to learn the
language of theology, i.e., to learn how to talk about God!

The Spirit at work in our unconscious

There is an intriguing relation between my conscious will and my bodily functions which operate unconsciously.

Take the heart beat. Shouldn't we have some control over something so essential to our life? But we do not.

Take sleep: why can't I will to sleep? It seems as though something so vital for human life would be under the conscious control of the will. But it is not.

Sexual desire is similar. It arises willy-nilly. My body functions on its own terms, beyond my voluntary control.

Isn't there a parallel here with the Holy Spirit working in our life? Should we not recognize that the Spirit is always with us and in us, yet often working independently from our consciousness? That Spirit operates on its own terms, beyond our control.

What can I do but stand in awe and wait on God!

Prayer service for healing

We were having a prayer service for a friend deathly ill with cancer. I couldn't help but feel uneasy when some prayed, "We know you will work a miracle in our friend's life and rid her of this cancer." When my turn to pray came, I simply said, "God, we cannot dictate to you; we cannot manipulate you, but we are confident of your healing presence with our friend right now."

Sometimes God works miracles, but the fact is that more often God does not work spectacular miracles in cases such as advanced cancer. Can it be right to build up hopes for something that is not ours to control or to know?

But the friends' praying for a miracle forced me to examine my faith. Do I take my position just because I don't have complete faith in the God for whom all things are possible? The Scriptures exhort us to pray for healing and remind us that God can work miracles. So I pray for healing, but leave the results up to God.

Tapestry or whiteboard

Sometimes life seems like a rich tapestry, and sometimes it seems like a whiteboard on a classroom wall. Sometimes there seems to be depth, beauty, and warmth in everything, and at other times all is a bland, blank icy surface. Perhaps these are the times described by the mystics as the "dark night of the soul."

These contrasting subjective states might well have something to do with the functioning of the brain and glands in our body. Therefore we should not directly link them to such sentiments as "God is close to me," or "God has forsaken me," as we are wont to do. Perhaps we should try rather to appreciate the multi-faceted nature of our inner life. Does your life feel like a tapestry?

Is activism non-Lutheran?

I once made an announcement in our local church inviting participation in the forthcoming Memorial Vigil to be held in commemoration of the anniversary of the Iraq War, and was criticized for making that announcement.

One result of that little episode was that it fostered an altered sense of my own identity, because I had taken a small step toward encouraging a public stand on the issue of peace and war, and received criticism for it. I'm not sorry I did it.

Why is a Memorial observance and a peace vigil questionable? Is even such mild "activism" inappropriate for a church to be involved in? Why should a Lutheran Church not take a public stand on issues of peace and justice? How can we follow the footsteps of the Old Testament prophets and of Jesus Christ without raising our voice for justice and peace?

The lowest common denominator

People of the Old Testament period—Israelites, Jews, the "Chosen people"—lived by the Gospel just as we in the Christian era do. How is that? Because the essence of the Christian Way is to hallow the name of God, i.e., to believe and love and obey the one, true, invisible Spirit-God.

That starting point hasn't changed, and that is still the lowest common denominator between Judaism and Christianity. Jesus made that Way clearer, richer, more intelligible by the way he lived and taught and used his whole life.

The worship of the invisible spiritual God, who in various ways manifested the divine will in ethical guidance and moral demand was what set Israel apart from her neighboring countries and cultures. In the Christian era we still worship that same God and pray, "Thy will be done" in our lives and behavior.

This should serve to set the community of believers apart from the secularism that surrounds us today, as it set Israel apart from its pagan neighbors.

The unsophisticated Jesus

Jesus was an unsophisticated man of his times, having little knowledge of science, philosophy, world history, art, etc. So he simply called God his "Father." Some of his sayings may seem naïve to us. But God's power was working in this simple, humble, trusting young man who was answering the call of God at the time of his baptism. And so God was able to do extraordinary works of power through him.

Contrast such an approach to Jesus with statements of the creeds and liturgies of the church. There we have put Jesus in the mold of the "second person of the Trinity," "eternally begotten of the Father...Light from Light, true God from true God, begotten not made, of one Being with the Father...." Which statements come closer to the picture of Jesus drawn in the Gospels of Matthew, Mark and Luke?

Second Week   Wednesday   *Prayer*

Prayer at surgery

Before surgery I had the strong, assuring feeling of Jesus as the Great Physician standing over me and working with the nurses and doctor. I felt relaxed and assured that God was above me, around me and in me. It gave me a peace that no matter what might happen all is well. What a blessing to be able to go through surgery in that calm frame of mind!

Next time you're having a critical experience, try quieting yourself with deep breaths and a prayer something like this: 'God who made my body, I now commit it to you again. Let your Spirit flood my body and also flood the hands of the surgeon, and let there be peace.

Second Week   Thursday   *The Way*

What are the big issues?

The issues that propel the religious right seem to be abortion, homosexuality, and prayer in schools. Important as these might be, they are definitely not the primary moral issues of our day.

Nuclear weaponry, spending nearly half of our national budget on waging wars, the bondage of our government to the wealth of corporations, the gap between the obscenely rich and the desperately poor, and such matters are of far greater import for the welfare of humanity.

What would Jesus do if he were to visit Washington or Wall Street today? Or, the more relevant question, What would he have us do?

Plant intelligence

Are not plants, with their lavish foliage and flowers, more beautiful than human beings, who, by comparison, lack color and show only slight variation from one to another? And maybe the plants are equally "intelligent"— and this is not to deny the function of DNA and all the other scientific explanations.

Just consider the miracle of how plants are able to produce their symmetry and color with startling uniformity year after year, going from seed to stalk to flower—and in many cases to delicious fruit—season after season after season. Do we fully appreciate this "intelligence"?

What do human beings have that plants don't have? We have reason, sight, speech, mobility, and self awareness. Maybe that's about it for the human race! But do we fully appreciate these distinctively human gifts?

Is evil forever?

There must either be an eternally opposing force to God and the Good—it may be called evil power/Satan/Devil — or there is an eternal tension within God's nature between a life force and death force.

The Bible presents evil as being from the pre-history story of the Fall. Evil was the death force, so the ancients killed animals as offerings to appease God and redeem themselves.

Then God appeared in the person of Jesus, and the death force working in his generation killed him. But in the resurrection the life force again prevailed and this power is always available to all who call upon it.

But what about a final vindication of the life force? Must there not be a "happy ending" when the life force will clearly show its conquest over the death force? It is presumptuous for human beings to declare what form that conquest will take. But the images in Revelation, the last book of the Bible, give us a hint, not so much in its details as in its vast, cosmic images of a "new heaven and new earth."

We need a child's naiveté

Jesus said, "Anyone who will not receive the kingdom of God like a little child will never enter it." (Mark 10) What does it mean to receive the kingdom like a child? It can hardly refer to the quality of moral goodness. It is a statement about trust. If a child has been nurtured by a loving parent, that child never questions that the parent will take care of all his/her needs. Naïve trust is the most distinguishing characteristic of little children. We call Jesus God's Son, God's child, because he had complete and perfect trust in his Father.

And that is the attitude that we people of faith are called to cultivate—simple naïve trust that the Creator will take care of us and all will be well. But how hard it is for us adults who have become so tainted by doubt and cynicism and self-importance to embrace this child's attitude! God, help us to be naïve in our trust in you!

Forgiveness is painful

When there has been a serious breach between people and one bears a deep grudge against another, forgiveness does not come cheap. It is not appropriate to the gravity of the situation simply to say, "It's OK; let's forgive and forget." No, it is painful to confess; it is painful to forgive. I must sacrifice my wounded pride in order to forgive. Forgiveness is a "trial by fire."

This human interaction of forgiveness reflects that prototype of all forgiveness that is found in the Christian Gospel, namely, that forgiveness comes through the cross of Jesus Christ—through a trial of bloody suffering.

Love of God and self

Despite the usual Christian call for sacrificing one's self in order to live for and love God, love for God and love for self are inextricably related. When I say, "I hate God for all this misery," I am also saying, "I hate myself." But when I can joyfully say, "I love God," I realize I love my life and myself.

This experience makes Carl Jung's interpretation of God as being the most profound depth dimension of the Self more understandable. Try loving God in yourself today.

Who can be trusted?

I sometimes fall into an insecure vision of the world as a dangerous, uncontrollable place, a kind of ungrounded, unstable mass. Politicians, self-styled leaders, teachers and religionists all seem to be promoting differing and conflicting causes, each trying to persuade the masses to follow some particular brand of truth.

But which of them can be trusted? Who is speaking the truth, and which ones are speaking falsehood? Furthermore, does anyone really know for sure what is the truth? We can't even trust religion necessarily to be based on truth. And how about the Bible? Parts of the Old Testament are full of messages of divine commands to use cruelty and violence.

Where can we find an anchor, a solid rock, an absolutely dependable place to stand in the midst of the flow of history and current modern culture? Maybe we can't expect such security. Maybe we simply have to live looking upward moment by moment.

"The burning bush"

This great story from Exodus is pregnant with symbolic
meaning about God. The theophany (appearance of God)
was through a bush—the most commonplace, nondescript
thing one could find. But it was through that very
commonplace thing that the divine chose to appear. So with
us: God appears in the most unexpected places and speaks
in the most unexpected events at the most unexpected
moments.

The divine appearance was like fire—a flame—hot,
powerful, uncontrollable, both helpful and harmful to
human beings. A flame is momentary, disappearing as
quickly as it appears. It cannot be grasped and held.
Furthermore, you can see right through it—it appears to
have no material substance.

So with God: elusive, non-substantive, God is here
and then disappears; we cannot grasp and hold God, but
nevertheless a vital energy emanates from this divine
presence, a powerful energy that destroys and creates
and purifies.

How we would like to capture, preserve and
institutionalize the sacred moment, to encapsulate the
ecstasy of a fleeting sense of the divine presence. But
alas, that is impossible! The day's duties call; hum-drum
submerges us.

Jesus' "predictions" of his death

In the Gospels Jesus' "predictions" of his death actually mean that Jesus realized that his death would be inevitable; being inevitable, he could "predict" it. Why? Because one who so completely personified righteousness could not be tolerated by this world. None of humanity, myself included, really want to put God first in everything and love our neighbor as ourselves. So we get rid of the voice that calls us to that way of living. We stamp out this uncomfortable voice; i.e., we crucify the Son of God!

But Jesus came among us in spite of knowing the inevitability of a clash, and in that is his love for humanity—to be human, knowing that his life would have to end in a tragic climax!

"Not I, but the Spirit within me"

The biblical perspective on our everyday actions is, "I do it, yet not I, but the Spirit of God within me." This seems like a contradiction. How can we image such a paradox? It is as though our minds and bodies are all wired up for action, but without any electric current in the wires. The Spirit of God is that current which enables effectual work to be done.

Another image is a fine piece of art in a room but it can't be seen because the lights aren't turned on. The Spirit is the light. The Spirit is utterly non-material and hidden, yet it changes everything.

Where is happiness?

In Aristotle's philosophy happiness is the result of goodness. Do good and you will be happy. Flowers and bees can be happy, because they're fulfilling their goal, which is to bloom, to make honey, etc. Human happiness is more complex, because human will and choice are involved. When we will to do the good, then we find happiness.

Happiness does not depend on the good things people are doing for us. It is born from the good we are doing. So regardless of how difficult circumstances may be, how much suffering or sorrow we face, if we do the right thing in that circumstance, we will find happiness.

God, grant that I take the initiative, not to look for happiness, but to create happiness this day.

Time and change

I had been mulling over the abstract concept of time,
realizing that there is actually no reality to time at all.
But a meaning of time suddenly came to me while talking
with old Mr. Shiraishi at the Naganuma Language School in
Tokyo, where we studied Japanese language some 60 years
ago.

I felt deep emotion as we recalled the past as it related to
that school—from its existence in the primitive conditions
at Suidobashi, with our wonderful teachers and all the
friends we made in those smelly classrooms situated above
the dirty river with its freight barges carrying away Tokyo's
"night soil."

Then we looked around us and saw the vast changes in
the neighborhood of the present location of the school in
Shibuya, where splendid, tall buildings are closing in on
either side of the new school building.

At that point it struck me that time is change. Time is
what transpires as change takes place. Change requires
time. Time can be measured by the degree of change taking
place, whether that be changes in my body ("growing old")
or changes in the physical culture, or changes in the earth's
topography through millions of years.

Ninth Month

Australian landscape

Watercolor, 2010

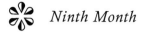

First Week   *Monday*   *Kingdom of God*

God's Kingdom in conflict

There is currently an increasing trend among biblical scholars to understand that the concept of "Kingdom of God" was used by both Jesus and Paul in contrast to and opposition to the Roman Empire of their day. It was Jesus' way of saying that final allegiance belongs to God and not to the Roman government. It was Paul's way of saying that Jesus, not Caesar, is Lord. When the early Christians acted out their faith in this way of recognizing only God as their final authority for thinking and acting, conflict and persecution by civil authorities often broke out. The Book of Acts narrates many such conflicts.

What does this say about the relation of religion to politics? What does this say about us Christians today and occasions of conflicting loyalties between Christian teaching and civil policies?

Are we ready to announce our loyalty to principles of the righteous Kingdom of God in the face of unjust, oppressive, or violent policies of our government?

First Week   *Tuesday*   *Jesus Christ*

To believe in Jesus is a way of life

To "believe in Jesus" means we believe Jesus truly did show us God's true character—God's rejection of wrong-doing and passion for justice for all, based on inclusive, forgiving, love. Therefore, love is at the center of the universe, because Jesus showed God, the center of the universe, to be love.

Then love must rule our life! Believing is not believing a Being out there is almighty, all-knowing, eternal, etc. It is not believing a concept to be true, or believing that a certain doctrine is the right way to think. No, it is a way of life. Lip service to certain doctrines is not what believing means!

Lord, help me to prove my faith, not by talking the talk, but by walking the walk with you today. I want to join the crowd of people on the Way.

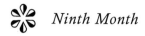

First Week   *Wednesday*   *Human condition*

The prophets' message to us

The prophets of the Old Testament faced such a different society than ours that it is natural that their message often doesn't really "fit" us. E.g., nobody in American society is bowing down before carved wooden idols.

However, our generation has certainly forsaken the invisible God as much as the Israelites did. So we must ask, "What are the alternative gods of our generation? The visible, tangible god of Materialism? The god of Militarism?" Is there any doubt that we put more trust in military defense than in the providence of God?

The nation of Israel was based on theocracy, i.e., God was supposed to be at its center. Although "In God we trust" is engraved on our coins today, in reality, is not the ideological foundation of our nation a capitalism based on making profit? And, predictably, the moral result is greed. We need the prophets' message today as much as the people of Israel needed it 2500 years ago!

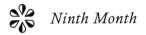

First Week *Thursday* *Faith*

The flux and the rock

Our emotions are in constant flux. All human feelings and experiences are always in flux, flowing like a river, tossing us about, as the Buddhist tradition emphasizes. But, although Process Theology would shy away from this figure, God is a rock!—to use a figure so often used in the Psalms. God is absolutely dependable, unchangingly trustworthy.

So it is best not to focus on emotions, which wax and wane. Emotions are deceptive for, in the long run, they actually have no reality. May the Lord help us to stand on the Rock today!

First Week *Friday* *Reflections*

"I don't know"

A Christian British scientist interviewed by Bill Moyers on TV suggested God is like the fifth dimension of existence: there are the three dimensions of space, plus the fourth dimension of time, and then a fifth dimension of spirit, about which science knows hardly anything.

He said science and faith meet in the attitude of humility that admits "I don't know." Good science and good religion should both start with that. We are all small, finite and limited in all five dimensions. Only the arrogant one dares to say, "I know."

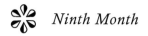

Second Week   Monday   *Kingdom of God*

Kingdom of heaven is where?

The Kingdom of heaven and the Kingdom of God are generally considered to be synonymous. Some interesting ideas follow from this premise, for if God is everywhere present in the universe, so is heaven everywhere present. Then if Christ ascended into heaven, he ascended into a universal sphere and is a universal presence. Christians believe in this universal presence of Christ.

Then what does it mean for us to "go to heaven" when we die? Heaven is everywhere; heaven is here, now. So does death usher us into the spiritual state of heaven in which we become, with God, everywhere present?

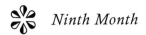

What is a witness to Christ

Love is the core of Christian faith. As such it should lie at the very core of our being and doing, and show itself in our basic attitudes. If my intention is to express my faith in daily living, then all my conversations and actions will somehow be an expression of love.

Some Christians emphasize the importance of making a verbal "witness to Christ" as a form of trying to convince people to believe in the Gospel. But such talk about religious matters does not necessarily express the core of our being and the basic attitudes which reveal that core. The language of such "witness" can be merely superficial verbiage.

The language of everyday conversation is what really expresses our basic attitudes. Such language is the genuine expression of our faith and witness. We should use the name of Christ not to advertise our Christian affiliation, but as a reference to the source of love—God's love and our love.

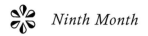

Training in prayer

I reaped several insights from the retreat on "Healing through Prayer" led by Mark Dahle. He was extremely pragmatic and down to earth in the practice of prayer, especially intercessory prayer, or prayer for others. Here are some of his helpful thoughts and practices.

Prayer is a skill; practice it and see what works. If nothing happens, try a different approach until you find a way that does work. Just knowing someone is praying for me, apart from any other effect of the prayer, is a comfort and support.

Praying for someone else gets me out of navel-gazing and is an expression of love for others.

The focus of my prayer for others must be on the other person and on God, not on the adequacy of my own intercession.

Focusing on the other broadens my horizon, broadens my caring, and broadens the scope of my love.

Verbalizing our needs to say a prayer is a value in itself. The prayer that acknowledges the presence of God in everything that happens—in sickness and in health—is comforting.

When I pray coincidences occur; when I stop praying coincidences stop occurring.

I need to practice the art of praying more diligently!

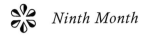

Jesus and the eunuchs

In the light of the intense debates going on in the churches today, which is of such magnitude that issues of homosexuality are actually splitting many churches, we might do well to pay close attention to the one instance where it seems to me that Jesus is saying something relevant to homosexual persons.

It is a passage about eunuchs, men who do not have the capability of sexual activity with women (so that they were entrusted with keeping the harem of a monarch in that period of history). I wonder why this passage is not referred to in the vast amount of literature produced on the subject of homosexuality and the Bible.

This passage is found in Matthew 19:12 in the context of a conversation between Jesus and his disciples on the subject of marriage and divorce. The basic issue in the debate over homosexuality seems to boil down to the physiological question: is this type of sexuality innate nature for some people, or an acquired style of life that needs to be changed? Does this saying of Jesus shed light on this crucial question?

Because it is of such importance, let's look at several translations of this verse from Matthew. First, the King James version, where it reads, "There are eunuchs who were born thus from their mother's womb, and there are eunuchs who were made eunuchs by men...." The New International Version reads, "Some are eunuchs because they were born that way...." And, always original, The Message translates it: "Some, from birth seemingly, never give marriage a thought."

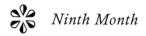
Although these descriptions were stated in the context of talk about eunuchs, it cannot be denied that at the same time they also constitute a "functional description" of homosexual persons, and clearly allow that some people are by nature not interested in heterosexual coupling. If that is the case, Jesus would hardly allow us to pin the label "sinful" on persons who are homosexual by nature.

Second Week   Friday   *Reflections*

Just to live is startling

I love these terse words of Emily Dickinson: "To live is so startling it leaves little time for other occupations."

Dickinson is calling us to wake up and be aware of our world and especially aware of all that is involved in "living"—our mind, our body, our emotions, our behavior, our relationships, our imagination, our dreams, our potential, our weakness, and so much more. To become sensitive to all these things and appreciate them is a full time job!

Are you startled at living today?

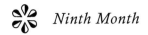

Third Week   *Monday*   *Nature of God*

No room for cynicism

The God of the cosmos is the God of my heart. This God, who is the Ground of all being, the God inherent in all time and space, is infinitely vast.

By contrast, this little being called "me" is infinitely tiny and insignificant, like chaff tossed around by the wind Yet—amazing grace!—the "Hound of Heaven" keeps chasing me.

The only fatal sin is cynicism, which denies both the divine possibility and the human potential. To be religious is to believe that even I am caught up into the infinite arms of the God of the cosmos. To be Christian is to believe that the God of the cosmos actually loves even me.

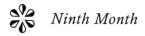

Third Week   *Tuesday*   *Jesus Christ*

It is hard to say, "Jesus is Lord"

"No one can say 'Jesus is Lord' but by the Holy Spirit" is
a hard saying. I believe that what it means is that faith is
indeed a gift—not in any everyday give and take sense, but
as a very existential, subjective experience. Truly to believe
the presence of the invisible God and commit to God is not
something a reasonable person is willing to do; it seems to
be a foolish thing. To do so is defying natural law; it is like
jumping off a cliff and expecting to be saved by a thread
tied to ones big toe!

So who does truly live by faith? Only the one whom the
Spirit touches and inspires with the reality of this invisible
One. I would be uneasy about committing myself to the
Jesus way if it were not for this nudging of the Holy Spirit.

Law and Gospel

People sometimes poke fun at Lutherans for giving prominence to the old formula of Law and Gospel. I admit that it smacks of 17th century Lutheran orthodoxy. I myself have generally not given it much thought. However, the polarity of Law and Gospel does point to some significant insights.

For instance:

1) A sermon should not be primarily "We should/ought/ must do so and so." If this predominates, the sermon becomes little more than ethical admonition, like a Rotary Club pep talk. This is "Law."

2) Neither should a sermon be entirely the story of what Jesus did—how he was a divine teacher and healer and died for the sins of the world. If this predominates, the sermon becomes little more than a history we are asked to believe. "Gospel," at its worst, can be just that.

3) A good sermon is a balance of both of these and shows how they work in a cycle. It shows how behavior ("Law" i.e., the right way of life) flows as a response of gratitude and commitment for the amazing love of God for us shown in Christ ("Gospel").

4) Bringing these two elements—which in essence deal with God's love for us (Gospel) and our love for neighbor (Law)—together in their right cause-effect relationship is the preacher's task. This makes the Christian message clear and applies it to life in a dynamic rhythm.

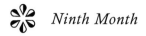

Third Week   *Thursday*   *The Way*

Going to heaven or following Jesus?

Pious Christians are prone to say, "Believe in Jesus and you'll go to heaven when you die." But the Bible really doesn't say much about "going to heaven." It says much more about following Jesus now. The scene described in Matthew 24 separating the sheep and the goats on the basis of whether or not they showed compassion has the clear message, "Follow the way of Jesus and you will stand blameless before God in the final Judgment." Subscribing to an article of belief is not the way to heaven

---

Third Week   *Friday*   *Reflections*

"Don't work so hard!"

Sometimes I hear the exhortation, "Don't work so hard; you're retired!" but I find it difficult to respond positively to that exhortation. For if I can't be working at something that is of service to others, or to the church, or to humanity, it is difficult for me to find meaning in my continued existence. I want to wear out, not rust out. How about you?

Varieties of salvation

If we study the history of cultures and the philosophy
of religion, it is plain that world views and religions of
different cultures and societies have developed in vastly
different ways. Each of them grows out of a different aspect
of the complexity of human thought and behavior.

Some societies—like ancient Israel—were very moralistic.
They had a strong sense of right and wrong, pure and
impure, etc., so they needed to find a way to relieve their
conscience when they offended the moral sense. They
found that sacrifice of another life—of an animal that
substituted for their own life, appeased their conscience
and supposedly pleased their God.

Other cultures, as some Asian (Buddhist) cultures, did not
have the same rigid moral sense. In this milieu the tendency
was to accept all behavior as long as it was not harming
other people. The principle was not so much to be right
and pure as to "live and let live." Escape or release from
the world with all its anxieties and desires, and quietly
meditating on the meaning of the "now" was the road to
salvation for them.

Is the Asian way to be condemned, or is God's finger to
be found in both streams of religious culture?

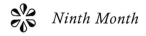

Fourth Week   *Tuesday*   *Jesus Christ*

Incarnation and death

This Christmas, the month in which my mother died, the Incarnation takes on a wider scope of meaning. It means that God experiences and accepts our human life in all its aspects—including death! For death is simply the back side of birth.

When the Gospel of John says that "the Word became flesh," (John 1) this assures us that the Word (the eternal Christ) accepts our human life in its glory and in its weakness, in its beginning and in its ending—in the vigor of youth but also in old age, sickness and death. What comfort there is in this!

Fourth Week   *Wednesday*   *Faith*

Introspection

Some people are always examining their spiritual life. Introspection is a good thing, but to be too introspective and bound up in concern about one's spiritual state can be anything but a virtue. Constant introspection is self-centeredness, and can be just as perverse as pride and arrogance. It can also lead to a self-induced neurosis.

So when thoughts of doubt and self-condemnation thrust themselves upon us, we should not indulge ourselves by focusing on these feelings, but cast them aside and concentrate on external matters—other people and their needs, the day's work, etc. Is not the essence of Jesus' teaching to focus on others rather than on ourselves, on serving our neighbor rather than navel-gazing?

No "cheap grace"

It is easy to rely on "cheap grace," thinking of forgiveness in terms of a daily prayer, saying, "Forgive my sins for Jesus' sake." That makes everything OK, so we can start the next day with a clean slate, knowing that we will dirty it again with careless or selfish behavior, but thanks to the forgiveness awaiting us every night, such sins are no big deal. Such an attitude takes the reality of sin and the reality of forgiveness much too superficially.

The real sin is the sinfulness of taking for granted that God's unconditional love allows us to live as we please, the sinfulness of our failure to reflect and examine our life, the sinfulness of participating in a society that perpetrates injustice and violence and destruction on a vast scale.

These things are not bits of dirt that blemish an otherwise clean slate. We can be saved from this sin only by a gracious God who permits us to live under the divine umbrella of constant forgiveness.

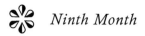

Sinners, but saints

In the biblical narratives the faults and grave failings of the great personages of the Bible are portrayed with remarkable frankness. Take King David—a giant in Israel's history, yet his scandalous affair with a married woman and deadly plot against her husband is written in great detail. Or Peter, the rock on which the Church is built. He betrayed Jesus three times on the very night when his support was most needed.

So why are these figures looked upon as saints and heroes, when they had miserable failures no different from any other human being? Obviously not because they were perfect, but because they saw their failures as sin, and repented of it. It was not that they had ideal behavior, but because the orientation of their lives was toward the ideal, i.e., their desire to be obedient to God. This is what made them saints and heroes!

Here is surely a model for us to remember as we evaluate human behavior, our own included.

Tenth Month

A fish if you wish

Oil, 2010

Avoid religion!

Religion should be avoided as much as possible, because it separates God from ordinary life and ordinary time. Religion tends to put God in a box of special ideas, special places, special times, special rituals, etc. Religion, as such, is one aspect of any culture. It is not necessarily a cradle for faith. It is more often a source of conflict and, as we know in today's international scene, even violence.

But if God is truly the all-pervasive Spirit in all of creation, God belongs not in a separate cultural package, but in the center of daily activities, in sociological, psychological and scientific endeavors in the world. God is in our midst. This does not detract from God's holiness; rather, it makes all things holy.

God, help us to find our way through religion—to you!

A whole new creation

Resurrection—whether Christ's or ours—is not about the immortality of the soul, nor is it about a miraculous return of breath into a body that has been declared dead. It is about a whole new creation—a creation no less amazing than the first creation of human beings from dust.

Christ's appearance after his entombment left those whom he met in shock and disbelief. According to the record, he entered locked rooms and appeared and disappeared in mysterious ways. Likewise, we have no idea what form our new creation might take. Lord, prepare me for the big surprise!

First Week   *Wednesday*   *Church*

Am I purified?

The hymn sung by the praise group this morning was, "Purify me, purify me, Make me pure as refined gold." I was struck by how "un-Lutheran" this song is. Lutheranism tends to say, We are not pure, never can be, shouldn't expect to be.

The Lutheran Church sees the heart of the Gospel to be that we are accepted and forgiven just as we are, "worts and all," unworthy servants. I appreciate this emphasis on grace in Lutheranism, although I believe a balance between this emphasis and the striving for "refinement," which Lutheranism tends to neglect, is necessary for a balanced daily life.

Let us be thankful for the grace that constantly prods us to w ard purity, but accepts us even when we're not pure.

First Week   *Thursday*   *Faith*

Intention is enough

Honest intention is all that is asked of us when we come to God. If from my heart I intend to follow my Lord, if I honestly intend to be open to God, then God takes care of the rest.

God does not hold us to a certain standard of either spirituality or moral perfection. My intention—and effort—to move toward a better way is enough. I can do no more than turn my face toward God, and say, "Here I am; I'm not sure of the way, but I want to walk close to you." With that, I know everything will be all right.

Actions and meaning of actions

There are two aspects to all human activity—the activity itself, and the meaning of the activity. The activity itself is a physical and material kind of thing. Doing activities requires training and nurture of mind and muscles to accomplish the right actions.

We also have certain feelings that accompany the actions, pleasant or painful. The animals also share this part of our life. They, too, do actions and need training to accomplish their work, and some of the higher animals surely have feelings about their actions and the treatment they get.

What is distinctively human is the meaning we attach to actions. We inevitably attach some meaning to every action, some reason for it, some goal prompting it, some value in it. We ask, Why do I do this? What good, or ill, is born of this action? Should I or should I not be doing this?

Finding meaning, like the actions themselves, needs nurture and training. But this is a spiritual task, not a physical one, so it takes spiritual nurture. It takes time, time for reflection on and examination of the action, and for prayerful meditation focused on its value.

May God grant us to take time for spiritual nurture and probing beyond superficial appearances.

The original sin

The primal ("original") sin is to think that I am an absolutely independent, autonomous being with no obligation toward anyone but myself, with nobody toward whom I have responsibility. This is humanistic thinking, and fits well into the American individualistic ideal. But I see this as *hubris* (pride), defiance of the Creator.

I am called to "fear, love and trust" (Martin Luther's words in his Small Catechism) the One who made me, gave me life, gave me a world of beauty and abundance to live in.

The point of many of Jesus' parables is that we are "stewards" of the creation, not masters of it. Master of the universe and of my life, transform my proud independence into dependent humility.

Second Week   Tuesday   *The Cross event*

Was Jesus sent into the world to die?

We often hear a declaration of faith that uses words such
as these, which are almost a Christian cliché: "God sent his
Son to die for our sins." But let's think about the meaning
of that sentence.

It is true to say that "Jesus came to die," or that "God sent
his son to die," because to be perfectly obedient to God's
will in the midst of this greedy, power-hungry, prejudiced,
non-thinking, envious, unrepentant human context, death
was the inevitable consequence of his way of life.

The world, our society, ourselves included, cannot
tolerate such behavior and message as Jesus gave. He had
to be killed, killed as a sacrificial lamb because he perfectly
did the will of God. In doing that, he was perfectly fulfilling
the whole Law of God. Why did Jesus do this? Why did
God send him to do this? This was a gift, a special gift of
God to the human race.

So I understand the logic of saying "Jesus came to die."
However, I understand those words to mean something
quite different from the view of the atonement that sees
Christ's death as a sacrifice offered to appease a God whose
wrath over human sin must be mitigated with some kind
of blood sacrifice. This view of atonement is still reflected
in the liturgy and hymns used in many churches today,
including my own.

The reader is no doubt aware that many of the Tuesday
thoughts reflect my struggle to interpret the meaning of
Jesus' death.

I hope you too are willing to go beyond the clichés which
easily slide off our tongues and struggle with the meaning
of this earth-shaking event.

Second Week   Wednesday   *Church*

"We believe in the holy catholic Church"

This is what we confess in the creeds of the church. This
is a unique statement in the Apostolic and Nicene creeds,
because it is the only object of belief that is not a spiritual
reality, but an institution. Thus it seems out of harmony
with our basic statements of faith in God, Christ and the
Holy Spirit.

However, this very fact should point to the spiritual
nature of the church and remind us that the church is, in
essence, not an institution among other institutions, but
also is a spiritual reality. It is the "communion of saints,"
i.e., the spiritual bond among all believers.

But what then is the relation of that spiritual entity to this
organized congregation down the street that goes by "First
Lutheran"? We need to think seriously about the uneasy
linkage, so easily tattered, between the two. May God
give us the wisdom to create a genuine spirituality in our
ecclesiastical institutions!

It is too wonderful!

When we contemplate the vastness of God, it seems preposterous to believe that this God is the very object of my everyday faith. Can I actually be in touch with such a God? Impossible! But no, this One is the very object of our faith. Faith is such a wonderful thing, because we deliberately lay hold of this impossible reality, experience this impossible relationship. I challenge you to adventure into the impossible today!

The sexual orientation issue

God made us all different in every aspect of our existence, so there is no way we will ever all think alike or be alike. There will always be diversity. Thus, when we try to mediate between conflicting views in any arena, there's only one amicable solution, viz., to agree to disagree. The alternative is endless conflict, which is most unbecoming to any Christian community.

I think the only way for our church to solve the current conflict over sexual orientation is to take the "agree to disagree" stance. Practically speaking, that will mean allowing individuals, congregations and synods to take differing positions while amicably agreeing to disagree.

There is, however, still a big "fly in the ointment," and that is biblical interpretation. As long as some Christians take a fundamentalist position on Scripture interpretation, saying there are seven passages in the Bible that speak disapprovingly about homosexual behavior, and therefore homosexuality is sinful, there can be no "agreeing," because that is condoning sin.

So is not the basic issue for Christians in this whole matter how we interpret the biblical statements that refer to homosexuality? But that throws us back to the larger issue of Bible interpretation in general. Is what was written two or three thousand years ago to be taken as the absolute unchangeable "Word of God" chiseled in stone for all time? Or is God a living Presence through all of history continually speaking a fresh word to and re-forming the Christian community according to the dynamic guidance of the Holy Spirit?

One more thing: Both the church and society at large would be better off if the focus of concern would be shifted from heterosexual vs. homosexual orientation to sexual faithfulness vs. sexual promiscuity. In this lies the locus of moral problems on which we all need to work together.

God is in all and all is in God

A prominent theme in Process Theology is the belief that God is imminent in the world and the world is imminent in God. Therefore we can experience everything that happens as being in the plan of God. St. Paul prayed that Christians might be "filled with the fullness of God." (Ephesians 3) And, as we sing in the Eucharistic liturgy, "Heaven and earth are full of thy glory."

The difference between so-called "believers" and "non-believers" is that some people intentionally appropriate this wonderful working of God, strive to be constantly aware of it, and are thankful for it, and others intentionally reject it and are left to themselves, alone in the universe.

God, open my eyes to recognize you in and around me today!

The newness of the new covenant

When Jesus said, "Take and drink, this is the New
Covenant in my blood, shed for you and for many for
the forgiveness of sins," he was announcing a revolution!
This new covenant is something really new! It was not just
substituting the blood of Jesus for the blood of bulls and
goats to be offered to appease God.

No, Jesus hereby announced an entirely new system.
It was God showing his extravagant love for humankind
through the Incarnation. That is to say that God knew that
his way would be opposed by both religious and secular
leaders of the day, who would be so outraged by his way of
life and teaching that they would do away with him.

But God sent the gift anyway, in this special form of the
man Jesus. This "coming anyway" shows the profound
divine love that accepts sinners and forgives them. Sin
doesn't need to be "expiated" by a blood offering any more.
Sin is forgiven by accepting the gift of the Jesus event,
thanking God for that willingness to go all the way for the
sake of humanity, and then committing ourselves to the
way God has shown us through Jesus.

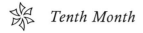

Third Week   Wednesday   Faith

Faith is a choice

I have faith if I think I have faith; I have no faith if I think I
have no faith. The difference between the two all depends
on whether I open myself to the reality of the unseen
love of God, or whether I doubt that reality, choose to be
indifferent to that reality, or defy that reality.

O God, faith is so elusive—so hard, so simple! Help us to
be open to the grace that encompasses us!

Third Week   Thursday   Commitment

Love God with your mind

The biblical injunction, "Love the Lord your God with
all your mind...." means to respond to God in rational
ways as well as intuitive and emotional ways. Rational
ways include thinking and planning our course of action
in accordance with what we have learned about God's
way from education, experience, etc. Only through such
thoughtful planning will our way of life actually be shaped
into the divine pattern.

We usually emphasize loving God with the heart. But
without the head being involved, that love can become
merely superficial emotion. Jesus said, "He who does the
will of my Father loves me."

Lord, I give myself , head and heart, to you this day!

The awareness of beauty

One of the wonders of our human potential is that we are moved by beauty. The colored leaves of December in Southern California against the deep blue sky, the snow-covered mountains creased by late afternoon shadows, and a thousand other phenomena that appeal to our senses—these many facets of nature we extol as being beautiful.

But with the passing of years, what is even a greater wonder is that we have this inner awareness of beauty which brings delight. This personal awareness makes us happy and makes life worthwhile. The subjective experience of beauty is as much a marvel as is the objective phenomena of nature that we call beautiful.

God, I thank you for this mystical awareness. Help me to nourish it in order to praise you all the more.

Fourth Week   Monday God

The "bottom line"

The bottom line regarding God in both Christianity and Judaism is that there is a God, and that this God is both transcendent—highly exalted above the universe, and immanent—intimately present in every human heart, and that this God cares passionately for humankind and all the created world.

It seems to me that this is the kernel of what the Bible—and all Christian theology for that matter—has to say about God. I want to keep close to the basics!

Fourth Week   *Tuesday*   *Who was Jesus?*

Incarnation

Think about the meaning of that central belief in the Christian faith: incarnation, i.e., God revealing God's self in the human flesh of Jesus. Here is the confluence of the divine and human, the heavenly and the earthly. And this is not just a description of Jesus Christ. It becomes a paradigm, a metaphor revealing the confluence of the heavenly and earthly, the supra natural and the natural in the whole created universe.

Because of the incarnation we see that the divine does infuse the human. In both the person of Jesus and the broader universe we see the mystery of this infusion, this "mix." The incarnation says that God is indeed in the world. The resurrected Christ says God is with us always. We believe the Holy Spirit is in us.

We must be aware of the fine line between God being in us, and God being identified with us. New age thought and many religions go over the line by identifying God and the self. Others tend to go over the line by distancing God too far from the world. That is, they tend to make God into a glorious, untouchable heavenly entity seated far above the universe and the human race.

Fourth Week   Wednesday   Faith

The miracle of life

All human beings are always surrounded by the divine
miracle of life—life in nature and in our body, and in our
spiritual self. To be religious, or to have faith is to be aware
of this divine milieu in which we live, to give thanks for
it, and to live constantly in joyful gratitude for life, for
humanity, and for the earth in all its beauty.

Fourth Week   Thursday   Faith

Faith is emptiness

Faith is the experience of emptiness—the emptiness of one's
mind and heart being open and uncluttered. Faith is the
stance of maintaining the mind as a free, smooth channel
by which the Spirit can glide into us. Faith is maintaining
ourselves as an empty vessel for the Spirit of God to fill.

Various spiritual disciplines can help us maintain that
mind-set. However, the paradoxical truth is that in the final
analysis that mind-set itself is a gift of the Spirit. Let us be
open to the Spirit's gifts.

Beauty and goodness

Beauty is that which has value for its own sake; goodness is that which has value for the sake of others. This is the distinction between an esthetic stance and an ethical stance.

It is pointed out that Eastern religion largely reflects the former, while Christianity largely reflects the latter. The main thrust of most of the Japanese new religions is to have a beautiful life—to be happy and grateful. In contrast, the main thrust of Christianity is to be active in love, to serve others and society.

The esthetic posture is centered in the philosophy of *eros*; the ethical posture is center in *agape*. However, both elements are necessary for a wholesome life. Without the passive, receptive stance of gratitude for all things and appreciation of the beautiful our life would be mechanical, cold and demanding. And without the active, giving posture of caring for others and society, reforming what needs to be changed, society would stagnate and gradually deteriorate

Eleventh Month

Fuku (pron. fookoo) (Japanese ideograph
meaning "happiness")

Oil, 2010

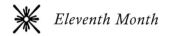

First Week   *Monday*   *The Kingdom of God*

The Kingdom is hidden

Many of Jesus' parables about the "Kingdom of God" can be found in the 13th chapter of Matthew. Some of these speak of the Kingdom as being hidden. It is an entity to be "searched for." The Kingdom of heaven is not obvious. It is not like a place on a map to which we can find our way and go at will. It is not a place we can enter by giving allegiance to certain doctrines or statements of belief.

Rather, it is a mysterious spiritual reality for which we must search, and which is so hidden that we often despair of finding it. But in these parables we are exhorted to continue the search. If we diligently do so, the promise is that we will find it.

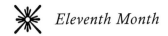

First Week   *Tuesday*   *The Cross event*

How forgiveness is related to the cross

That Jesus "came to die, had to die" are expressions of the fact that anyone who would stand firm in the way of truth and justice and love must inevitably, and with finality, clash with the evil forces of greed and pride and love of position and power in his society. That was the Cross experience.

Jesus realized throughout his ministry that people could not tolerate who he was; they would try to get rid of him. But regardless of the taunts, he was true to the God who sent him.

So it was the total event of Jesus' life that is God's gift of salvation. His attitude of forgiving love through his whole ministry, culminating in "Father, forgive them…" from the cross—this is the source of the forgiveness of sin.

The essence of sin is our human refusal to accept the incarnation, i.e., to acknowledge and accept who Jesus was. But of that Jesus says, "They know not what they do." In saying that, he accepts even our non-acceptance of him!

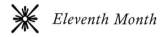

Agnostic praying

The very act of praying can itself be agnostic and displeasing to God, if I pray without confidence that what I am saying is heard. Praying with no confidence that I am being heard means that there is no value in prayer for me, and that my basic posture is one without hope.

So I must pray thankfully and joyfully, knowing God is hearing and answering in God's own good way. That means that I don't nag or try to manipulate God. I must say the prayer meaningfully from my heart once, and then say, "Thank you God! Amen." Too simple? Try it and see!

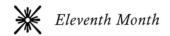

First Week   *Thursday*   *The Way*

The church and controversy

Many social issues are controversial. In that case what should be the church's stance? One way is to avoid the controversy and thus keep peace in the community. But why should not the church study the serious moral issues of the day, provide a safe place for discussion of them, pray together about them and try to find a line of action in accordance with the will of God?

Many people think it is best just to concentrate on worship and evangelism and leave social issues to the government. But how can Christians take that path when we remember how the prophets and Jesus fearlessly attacked the evils and hypocrisy of their day? Many church people say it is best just to entrust social policy to our government and go along with government policy.

But remembering the German church in the days of Hitler and the Japanese church prior to World War II, we must acknowledge that governments can be wrong. Churches in both of those countries have been apologizing to the world for their stance ever since.

The meaning of meaning

"Meaning" is a totally intangible thing, incapable of description, a completely non-material concept. Of what does meaning consist? I asked this question of meaning to a theologian recently and received the answer that meaning comes when one has a strong desire to do something, and then achieves it. Does "meaning" consist of purposefulness? But how do you make "purpose" concrete? Can we say it consists of commitment, to goals or to people? But "commitment," like the word "trust," is equally abstract.

Given this ambiguity, "meaning" is either a mental illusion, or a profoundly spiritual reality. Regardless of suffering, poverty, or miserable environment, if a person can find meaning in his/her existence, there can be genuine fulfillment and happiness. Conversely, when people, including the rich and famous, cannot find meaning in their life, not infrequently they cannot find a reason to continue living, become depressed, and end their lives.

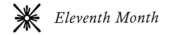

Second Week   Monday   *Nature of God*

God is not immutable

Many contemporary theologians believe God changes;
They see God as being not immutable.

Times change; customs and mores change; standards
of what is considered right and wrong change. In this view,
God does not stand apart from all this exciting process of
change and development, simply clinging to the immutable
stone tablets of some three and a half millennia ago. Rather,
God is in the change, influencing it and being influenced by
it. Recall that the Bible also speaks of God "changing
his mind."

God reveals God's self in a relevant way in every new
situation, and continuously works for positive change
within every situation. What happens if we apply this
understanding of God, rather than the written words of a
2500 year old text, to the current ethical problems that are
dividing our society and even our church, today? As just
one example, the last words of I Samuel 15 are: "The Lord
was sorry that he had made Saul king over Israel."

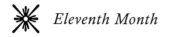

The *logos* is hidden in Jesus

The Greek word, *logos*, represents the divine outreach into the created universe, the expression of the divine character. This power of the divine outreach that created the world is ascribed to Jesus in the first chapter of John's Gospel ("the *logos* became flesh and dwelt among us"). This is John's philosophical foundation.

The same exalted descriptives are ascribed to Christ in Paul's letter to the Colossians. "He (Christ) is the invisible God, the firstborn over all creation. By him all things were created, things in heaven and on earth, visible and invisible…" (Col. 1). In both cases the phenomenon is similar—the divine appearing in nature and in humanity.

In both cases the divine is hidden in, with and under the visible and material. It takes the enlightened eyes of the soul to perceive the presence of God in the world.

This is why Christology is so perplexing, because the divine is so well hidden in the whole drama of Jesus' birth, life activities, death and resurrection. The essence of God is not obvious. Only those who sincerely search with an open mind and heart will find God in the person of Jesus.

Being vs. doing

"God, you are here," has been a good way to start praying. But it's getting a little trite and stagnant. The inner retort from God comes: "Yes, I am here; so what are you going to do about it?" Is there a better way to experience God than simply to sense the Presence?

Perhaps I should rather ask, "God, what should I be doing now?" Recall what comes after the petition to hallow God's name in the Lord's Prayer—"....Thy will be done."

God reveals himself not in static being, but in our doing the divine will. Can we say that doing God's will is doing the right thing in the right way, right now—doing what needs to be done for the common good. There is a dynamic challenge in this!

Outer conflict, inner conflict

Temptation can be either from external sources or from within. When we pray, "Lead us not into temptation," we usually think only of the external sources of temptation, of certain situations, certain unwholesome people or places.

But the internal sources of temptation are strongest and hardest to deal with. Predisposition and tendencies of the physical and psychic constitution are a relentless source of temptation. Excessive anger, lust or anxiety, and especially the hopelessness that comes with depression might be examples. These are indeed "thorns in the flesh."

If such "constitutional" sources can be healed by the medical or psychological professions, then the prayer to be delivered from temptation means that such healing should be sought. For needless temptations arising out of conflict which could be removed merely sap our spiritual energy through endless inner conflict.

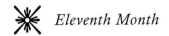

How fickle we are!

How self-centered, in-grown and fickle our perspective is! When the sky is clear blue, or when we have been made to feel happy for any reason, then we are grateful to God and think how good and close to us God is. When it is cold and rainy, or when we have a headache or feel weary, we doubt God's goodness, our faith weakens, and the song of praise wafts away.

How foolish! These subjective feeling factors—such as a clear sky or emotional ups and downs—have nothing whatsoever to do with the changeless majesty, grace and power of the eternal God.

Lord, give us a faith through rainy days, and hope even in troubled times!

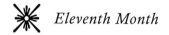

Embodied Spirit

If God's Spirit is not embodied in my body, including my mind and spirit, how can it be a reality for me? As I prayed today I had a sense that the Spirit needed a vessel to give form to the formless, and my body was the only vessel available. I remembered that St. Paul called our body "the temple of the Holy Spirit."

Lord, I thank you for this wonderful body, still in basically good condition after more than 80 years of living! Let me be aware of your existence in my total being today!

Third Week   *Tuesday*   *Jesus Christ*

Jesus' moment of ecstasy—and ours

The ninth chapter of Luke tells the story of Jesus' glorious transfiguration in the company of Old Testament saints on the mountain top. Peter's cry at that moment, "Let us build three tents for you to stay here! "(Mark 9:5) is so understandable. He wanted to encapsulate that mountain-top experience, to prolong it, to make it permanent. But the text says that the whole vision soon vanished, and they saw only Jesus.

We do not know exactly what happened on that mountain top, but Peter and his friends had a momentary glimpse of the glory of Jesus, different from his everyday, dusty appearance. Occasionally, like a pin-prick in the darkness, the glory of the Son of God whisks over us. "Stay, stay!" we plead, but alas, all is gone except a voice saying, "Just follow Jesus; that is enough."

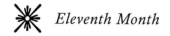

Born of a heavenly Being

"Our Father who art in heaven" expresses the mystery and paradox of the Christian concept of God. The One who is in "heaven"—that other entity nobody can define—this One Jesus called "Father."

"Father" is the metaphor of a person, a loving person, a provider, like us human beings. But at the same time this personal One is not living in our universe but is in another mysterious place—"heaven." Heaven must be very close to us!

This phrase also suggests that the one who gave us birth, our progenitor, our father originates in "heaven." It follows that my origins are in heaven, and our true nature is spiritual, of mysterious origin. Our human essence is born of a heavenly Being.

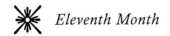

Third Week   Thursday   *Faith*

Despair vs. hope

The issue of productivity vs. non-productivity has always
presented a challenge to me. Productivity is the source of
meaning for my life. But this is not the deepest issue.
The deeper issue is despair vs. hope. When illness, bad luck
or accidents strike, I get thrown into non-productivity; then
I despair and wonder what use there is in living.

But maybe being productive is not all that important.
Neither God nor the world are dependent on what I can
produce. The more important thing is to maintain hope in
spite of everything. Hope honors God by believing in the
unchanging divine presence. That is true faith. The worst
sin is despair, for it says, "God no longer cares; God does
not hear; God is not there."

O God, as I experience inevitable diminishment of
productivity, give me grace to grasp onto hope for a
brighter future with you.

A pinpoint focus of broad meaning

When we were debarking from a cruise liner for a shore excursion, standing in an extremely crowded, narrow hallway of the ship, I had a revelatory moment when a tiny movement expressed a world of history and culture.

In my background are the packed commuter trains of Tokyo. Riding those trains force one into much more crowded conditions than we were in during that debarkation, and in those trains one learns to take body contact for granted. But in this situation on the ship, where we were quite crowded, I was not even aware that my body was apparently touching the body of a black woman next to me until she angrily spit out the words, "No pushing me around!" Of course, I apologized.

It is quite possible that she, as a black woman, had had experiences of being pushed around by whites, and taken advantage of as a woman by men. This long history of her culture and social reality was revealed in that moment of unintentional touching.

Such focal moments as that, in which a small word or gesture represent broad symbolic meaning, are of great interest to me. We never know what small, seemingly insignificant bit of our behavior might be such a symbolic moment for an observer. For better or for worse, many of those meaning-packed moments, especially if they occurred during the early years of life, tend to stick in our memory for a life-time.

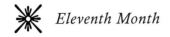

Fourth Week   Monday   *Nature of God*

Either deny or stand in awe

If we think deeply about the implications of the concept
we name "God"—that God is eternal, everywhere present,
all-knowing, almighty, loving creator of the universe—we
either have to deny the notion of God entirely, or stand in
awe of this God.

Most Christians waver between denial and awe, and
never honestly confront themselves and their religion,
probably because it is too uncomfortable to face the choice
between these two life stances—denying the existence of
God, or acknowledging with awe the existence of God.

May God help us make that life-changing decision, not
just once, but day by day.

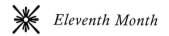

Fourth Week   *Tuesday*   *Forgiveness*

Sin and forgiveness—then and now

In reading an article in the Lutheran theological journal, "Currents" (vol. 36), on the "Aha Experiences" of Martin Luther, it was clear that the whole focus of Luther's spiritual experience was his discovery of forgiveness of sins. Finding forgiveness of sin not through meritorious works but through grace and faith was Luther's great "aha experience." That was truly a great discovery for him in the 16th century context of fear of an angry, punishing God whose favor could be found only by buying a ticket promising forgiveness for his sins.

But often it seems that this is where many churches "hunkered down" ever since that time. In the 16th century milieu there was a vivid sin consciousness, and Luther's sensitivity led him to have a dreadful fear of the righteous God. However, the world view of 21st century people is not one that is hung up on either the sin question or the concept of a wrathful God. Our generation glosses over the idea of sin and doesn't even like to use the word, except liturgically in church.

So Luther's world-view of primary emphasis on finding forgiveness of sin in the face of a wrathful God—this focus does not speak to today's world. Could that be one reason why many denominations are decreasing in numbers these days? Their language is not understood by the current generation. Perhaps their well-meant message, born out of the 16th century milieu, is not relevant to modern society's view of the human condition. Perhaps many traditional church bodies today do not understand the vocabulary of the contemporary cry of spiritual hunger.

Why do I need forgiveness?

We might think that our moral choices, right or wrong, are only a matter concerning myself and my neighbor. What does God have to do with my choices? This petition tells us that God does have something to do with my moral choices.

The implication is that when we have made bad choices, in some way we have offended against our Maker, who has a better plan for our lives. So we need to implore our Maker's forgiveness.

It is also significant that the statement is not "If you have sinned," but rather "Forgive my sin." The assumption is that I haven't been what I should be; I've not been perfect; I've made some bad choices. What to do? The only real solution lies in forgiveness, so that we can make a fresh start tomorrow.

Fourth Week   *Thursday*   *Faith*

Internalizing religion

The 6th chapter of John's Gospel is about bread and the body of Jesus, who said "You must eat my flesh." These are strange words. What do they mean? Do they not state a bold metaphor for the internalization of religion? " Digest what you hear; let it become a part of you; make it your own; don't just see it or listen to the words or learn them with your head; bite into them!"

Our pastor used this illustration in his sermon last Sunday: a book can be left on the coffee table as an attractive object to look at; that does nothing to us or for us. But if we read that book thoughtfully, it becomes internalized and changes our way of thinking and acting.

The former—just believing—can easily become "cheap grace," and of course the latter can become mere "legalism." Neither "believing" by itself nor "following" by itself are the proper motivation for Christian living. There is an overarching imperative that simply says, "Follow the way of Jesus because that is the right way, the true Way, the Way of Life; what happens after death we leave to our Maker."

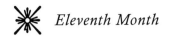

My philosophy

There is a philosophy undergirding every theology. This is obvious in the case of John Cobb, whose theological orientation is process philosophy. Kierkegaard's theology was based on a philosophy of existentialism. Paul Tillich's theology was based on a theology of culture. Some say that Karl Barth's theology was not satisfactory because it tried to avoid a philosophy.

One aspect of my own undergirding philosophy is a philosophy of language. I believe that language cannot define reality in any ultimate sense. Rather, language suggests reality through symbols and metaphoric expression, and gives images that attempt to describe aspects of reality. But mere sounds (words) can never convey the full scope of reality.

It follows that no amount of verbal definition and doctrine can grasp the ultimately "correct view" of theological matters, whether that be a definition of God, or of the Bible, or of the meaning of the Cross of Christ. It follows that I believe the proper stance is that of the perennial seeker after truth. I believe that we must hold doctrine lightly and humbly rather than with the arrogance of overconfidence.

Twelfth Month

Commissioning of Rev. H. Tokuhiro,
missionary from Japan to Brazil

Oil, 2009

Dealing with the law of self-preservation

There is a great, universal sorrow in the world, sadness over the suffering of all the created universe, because it decays, it dies. (Cf. Romans 8) The whole family of created beings, especially animals and humans, live by the law of self-preservation. If they didn't have this instinct, they would die.

Each creature must struggle for its own self-preservation. And this in turn causes a conflict that works against the sustainability of the whole.

Therefore, God's chosen Servant Jesus also suffered in his historical life. It was the demand for preservation of their own status and livelihood of themselves and their institutions that created the conflict between Jesus and his opponents.

But Jesus did the unthinkable—he endured the accusation of his killers, "He saved others, let him save himself." He overthrew the law of self-preservation with a higher law— the way of self-sacrifice.

The Christian transformation is the process of turning from focus on self-preservation to focus on preservation of the whole. This radical reversal of values upsets the way of the world. It is a way that inevitably leads through suffering.

Why three days in the tomb?

Where was Jesus from Good Friday afternoon until Easter Sunday morning? Why such a long wait for the resurrection? Did Jesus have a task to fulfill during that time—something that actually "took time" on the divine clock? The old creeds spoke of the "descent into hell." Did that trip take time?

Or was it to give time on the human clock for his dead body to begin to decay? Only thus could human beings know for sure that his post-resurrection self was indeed a complete transformation of the molecules composing his body, that his resurrection was not a "trick," but was indeed a new creation.

Worshiping is a task

It was never intended that a worship service should entertain a passive congregation of observers. Worship is work—the work of active listening, lively participation, and whole-hearted commitment. I get nothing from the hour of worship if I don't work at it, with attention and active listening.

I think the Lord will forgive us if we work on the Sabbath—if that work is worship!

A morning prayer

O God, here I am in your presence.

Thank you for the great world in which I was born.

Let me tread this planet with gratitude and joy today!

    Broken vessel that I am

Use even my brokenness this day.

Take away all barriers to the free flow of your grace

    into my life and through my life today.

Remind me throughout this day, over and over again,

    to be aware of your goodness and guidance!

Amen

Words—printed, electronic, divine

The written, printed word exists in space; we know where to find a certain piece of data. The book, the paper has a place in space.

But the electronic word of an internet site, on which we depend more and more, exists not in space but in time. We make it appear out of nowhere, and it disappears again into nowhere. It is here now and gone in a split second.

We might say the first mode describes an art gallery, while the second describes a music concert. The first is a visible, material, relatively permanent collection of things; the second is an invisible, non-physical, momentary impression on our ear drums.

I wonder which best describes the mode of the "Word of God"— printed page or electronic communication, museum or concert?

Second Week   Monday   *Nature of God*

The mystery of light

One of the great mysteries of this marvelous universe we live in is the mystery of light. What is light, anyway? We take for granted the difference between light and darkness, but that says nothing about what light really is. We look at the sun, or at a candle, and see what we call light. But if you were to dissect the sun, or the candle flame, would you find some essence called light?

We know light by what it does to the things on which it shines. In the night a light makes the invisible visible. So what has the light done to those objects to make them visible? Has it sent a ray to change the nature of the object? If, as scientists say, light is likely a wave, or possibly an emanation—either is equally mysterious!—why doesn't the wave appear as light, rather than the object on which it falls? But we are told that the space between the sun, from where these waves come, and the earth or other planets, moons, etc. is total darkness.

I'm not a physicist, so these are just a common man's musings. But when the Bible describes God and also Jesus as "Light," I have similar thoughts. We can't see the divine emanation, or the "waves" of the Spirit, but what that divine energy does to the persons on which it falls makes the difference of darkness and brightness. I want to "walk in the light!"

Jesus' teaching in a nutshell

Surely Mark put some of the most significant, all-embracing sayings of Jesus in chapter 12, one of the last chapters of his Gospel and the final sayings before the Passion and death. And what is the long parable here that incites the religious leaders against him? It is the parable of a landlord leaving his vineyard to servants, sending his ambassadors to call these servants to account for their stewardship; but the servants beat and kill the ambassadors, including the son of the master. (The listeners identify this son with Jesus.)

What is the significance of this final parable? Is it not that the final purpose of the prophets and Jesus was to remind people that they are only stewards of property belonging to the Owner. I.e., they came to bring God's perspective on what life is all about: It is about the human race being stewards and caretakers—not owners—of all the earth's resources and all our potential. In the end we will be called to account for our stewardship, account for how we have used what was entrusted to us.

So this is what Jesus was all about, viz., bringing the presence of God into the world and reminding us that all things ultimately belong to God, not to us. We have not created the elements of nature; they are a given. Neither have we created our own self. The spark of life is a gift. So the gist of Jesus' message was, Give priority and honor to your Maker and humble yourself before him!

But sadly, we, like the people of Jesus' day, do not like to hear that message.

Two movements in the Eucharist

The essence of the Sacrament of the Eucharist is also the essence of the entire Christian faith: In one and the same simple act, the act of "eating the Body of Christ," two distinctively different, indeed, contrary things happen. By ingesting the "Body of Christ" we participate in Christ's perfect sacrifice of his life for the fulfilling of the entire scope of "salvation history" as we know it from the whole Bible.

At the same time we participate in the new way of life God revealed through Jesus—the way of self-sacrifice for the sake of putting God first and obeying God's command to give ourselves up in a struggle for love and justice as Jesus did. I.e., we are simultaneously forgiven through the divine sacrifice of love, and thrust into the world to sacrifice for others.

Just three prayers

God doesn't need a lot of words from us. Just three short prayers are enough:

> Our Father who art in heaven,
>> hallowed by thy name!
>
> Come Holy Spirit!
>
> Thank you, God, for everything! Amen

What do I really want?

Jesus said to the lame man, "Do you want to recover?"
> (John 5)

These words strike at the heart of the matter.

He asks me today, "What do you really want?
> Do you want to change or not?"

The lame man made excuses, but no excuses were allowed.

Today I want to rise up on my feet and recover—

> No excuses. So help me God!

God of the nation

In the Old Testament God deals with the people, Israel—Israel as a whole nation, not as individuals in the nation. This is hard for us modern Western people to understand, because we are so oriented to individualism. Our whole concept of democracy is based on individualism—individuals coming together to work with and for each other and thus forming a community.

In reading the Old Testament prophets, we usually interpret what God said in an individualistic sense, applying their profound teachings and visions and promises to ourselves as individual persons. But the warnings and pleadings are addressed to God's "people," referring to the nation of Israel, to a community, not to an individual.

Therefore, is it not more appropriate to apply their message to God's "people" today, i.e., to communities? We should apply them to our local church, to the national church, to our primary group, whatever that might be, and to our city, nation and world. We must try to get into a different mode of cultural thinking, where the individual is subordinate to the social unit. Only then will we be able to understand the Old Testament.

Living several decades in Japanese society and experiencing the underlying collectivity consciousness, or "group think," of that culture proved to be a significant step for me in the direction of getting the feel of the social solidarity that underlies the Old Testament.

The "image of God" is personal

Most of us believe that human beings are created in the
"image of God," as stated in the Genesis creation story.
This is a descriptive of essential humanity. If that is so, then
God, whatever else God might be, is a personal God.

The problem involved in trying to conceptualize a
personal God is that "personal" means "person" and that to
us means a human being.

However, we cannot discover essential divinity or the
fullness of Godhood by saying God is in the image of
human persons.

"It is finished"

What is the meaning of these words from the cross? What is finished? The physical struggle of the execution? The "work of atonement"?

Was it not the mission of Jesus, the whole task of his life— his teaching, his bold witness to a new understanding of God, his fighting for the right, all of which culminated in the crucifixion—this was finished. We might say the Incarnation was finished.

At the moment of cruel death, we would naturally expect one to cry out, "Let it end quickly" or "I'm glad it's over," or "I ended in failure." But no—Jesus affirmed the goodness and meaning of the past thirty-three years. He saw his whole life, which inevitably culminated in death, as a task now finished.

This is a model for us. At the moment of death can we look back at the whole of our life in all its struggles and accomplishments and failures and say, "It is finished"?

The loving Presence

At the Sunday church service everything in the liturgy and hymns seemed to speak clearly of a God of goodness, of God's unconditional good, unconditional acceptance of the human race, yes, of me. I sensed that God is in everything, all around us, in the universe, in the earth, in nature, in this church, in my body and spirit.

Participating in Holy Communion deepened the experience—the Spirit of Christ in the bread, in the wine. One breathed in the sense that everything is good, everything is holy.

This was an experience of the love of God. It proclaims the truth that everything in the world is for us. That is what was revealed in the life and words and works of Jesus. But along that path that Jesus trod there was inevitable conflict with worldly powers. But Jesus willingly bore the consequences of that conflict, finally accepting even a humiliating death. In that act was the ultimate declaration of the unconditional love of God.

Praise God for God's unconditional love for the human race—and for me!

Third Week *Thursday* *Prayer*

When I am too old to "do"

I realize that my prayers are almost entirely stated in the form of "God, help me to do this or that." But does my life consist of only *doing*? Is it only in activities that I experience God at work in my life? If so, what will my prayer be when I am disabled or too old to do anything?

God is also relevant to my *being*. I had better start making being as well as doing the subject of my prayers. How about your prayers?

Third Week *Friday* *Reflections*

Social and individual perspectives

Judaism and the OT saw religion and the work of God in the world in terms of the social order, in terms of the Jewish nation. Jesus brought us back to the starting point of all things, namely, to the individual. Salvation is not for the prosperity of a nation, but for the individual to be right with God, right with him/herself, right with the neighbor.

Now is the era of the Church, and this is meant to be the age where the individual goes out to create and help and heal the social order again. Diagram these historical movements in terms of two funnels put together with their necks in the middle, with movement going from the social to the individual and back to the social in a new form.

Fourth Week   *Monday*   *Nature of God*

Israel's idolatry, and ours

The fundamental sin of Israel as pounded home by the prophets, such as Ezekiel, Jeremiah and others, was that they persistently went after gods of their own making, something they could see and touch, neglecting Yahweh, the true, invisible, spiritual God. Their complaint was that they had never seen this God!

But isn't this the sin of all of us—insisting on believing only something that can be scientifically verifiable? Like the ancient people of Israel, we feel that if only we could see, feel, hear, touch God, then we would be satisfied, and faith would come so naturally! Yet a God which would be so like ourselves that it could be grasped and understood by the senses would not qualify as the ultimate object of worship. Such a deity could not be the maker of heaven and earth.

The ultimate object of worship must be that forever invisible, forever elusive, forever intangible Mystery which is the source of life and the universe. Nothing else is worthy of worship, adoration and trust. This One is at once the most unreal and the most real thing in all existence.

That's why faith must be primary in the Christian religion. Faith is taking the risk of trusting in the reality of the unseen, unknown world. It is leaping, and then believing there is Someone there to catch us!

Yet, paradoxically, it is not a leap entirely away from this world. It is a leap into a different, hidden dimension of this world. Some call it the "spiritual" dimension, but the connotation of "spiritual" is too broad, too ambivalent, too much misunderstood. It is the mysteriously hidden dimension.

Resurrection power

It would seem that the power of God to bring life into the
dead body of Jesus is of a different order altogether from
the power necessary to make me live a full life today.
The former is a physical phenomenon, the latter a spiritual
matter.

Yet St. Paul constantly puts the two together and
interprets the resurrection as an existential event in people's
lives. He claims the spirit of the resurrected Christ dwells
in our spirit.

Is Paul thus "spiritualizing" the resurrection of Christ?
Or does this juxtaposition point to the common element
behind both—the incredible mystery of this mixture of
spirit and flesh called humanity?

History through the eyes of faith

Whatever human events the biblical writers experienced, they interpreted them as acts of God. Human beings appeared in history; the biblical writers say God created human beings. Moses saw a strange phenomenon in a bush; biblical writers say God was speaking through a fire, and that the ground by that bush was holy ground. Israel escaped from Egypt and wandered in the wilderness; biblical writers say God miraculously led the people of Israel out of Egypt and through the wilderness.

These biblical interpretations can be understood as seeing history through the eyes of faith. The "miracle" lies not so much in the events themselves, but in the way people interpreted the events. This interpretation does not mean that the writers "simply imagined" God was acting in these events or that they "simply made up a story."

No, we believe God is present in everything that happens in the world. To see that it is actually God working in creation and in saving a nation is an act of faith. It is the religious interpretation of history. Secular people, unfortunately, would not understand these events as acts of God, because they do not have the eyes of faith necessary to perceive that.

Heaven is not in the space-time order

Every time we pray the Lord's Prayer we acknowledge
a holy (hallowed, wholly Other) being who is personal
(Father). This One is "in heaven," that is, not a part of this
material order of existence. No human being knows what
"heaven" is. If it were a place, that would make it of our
own time-space order of things. It could not be even a place
out beyond this cosmos, because that would make God a
thing, filling space in some other territory. Such a being
cannot be what we call "God."

So this different order of existence must be God's order
of "spirit." Spirit is invisible to the human eye, does not
occupy space, nor is it limited by time. But because it is
such, it can infiltrate the created world and permeate the
human mind and body. So is not heaven in our midst here
and now? Hallowed be thy name!

Counseling as healing

During my days in the Personal Growth and Counseling Center in Tokyo I often said that Christian counseling is following Christ in a service of love through a healing ministry. This took on an even deeper dimension as I later reflected on my counseling career. Who came for counseling? It was the "sick," i.e., those with wounded hearts, painful feelings, hurting mind, bruised spirit, abnormal personality.

And how were these wounded people healed? Recall the story of the paralytic let down through a roof and the first thing Jesus said was, "Son, your sins are forgiven."(Mark 2) Why that seemingly strange response from Jesus? The weakness and wounds are sin in the sense of the original meaning of the word, i.e., "missing the mark" of health and perfection. So how does healing take place? The same way that Jesus healed—by offering "forgiveness of sin."

The counselor does indeed offer forgiveness, because the client casts his/her pain on the counselor, knowing that the counselor will bear it with him/her. The counselor yokes him/herself to this burden and empathizes—suffers with—the sorrowing client. The result is deliverance from despair. This empathetic acceptance is the dynamic of forgiveness.

Index

Index 238

V. A COLLAGE OF THOUGHTS (mainly on Fridays)

Reflections

Index 242